Praise for *Fanatically Formative*

"This book is a significant contribution to the early learning field—and deserves to be read and heeded."

—David Lawrence, Jr., President
The Early Childhood Initiative Foundation

"Bob Sornson makes it incredibly clear: Early learning success for our children is possible. Early learning success for our children is an essential ingredient for meaningful school reform and for the success of our nation."

—Jim Fay, Co-Founder
The Love and Logic Institute

"This is the missing link we've been looking for. Bob Sornson defines how we can transform our instruction to meet the needs of all children—one child at a time."

—Mark Tompkins, Superintendent
Harbor Springs Public Schools, MI

"Fanatically Formative describes all the pieces that must come together to give young children a quality learning experience with a commonsense approach. It is an engaging, thought-provoking, modern masterpiece! The ideas presented are essential to the success of school reform, enabling every child the chance at becoming a lifelong learner."

—Dawn Kemp, Special Education Teacher

"Educators know that the curriculum-driven instruction mandated today in our schools does not work for a very high percentage of students. How do we turn education around to be responsive to how students learn and ensure student success and lifelong learners who will become the leaders of tomorrow? Bob Sornson has elegantly put forth an answer that is at once both simple and profound, and takes the reader through the steps that ensure that every student and educator will succeed. Bob's compelling book, Fanatically Formative, is a must for all educators, especially those working with early learners. I consider it vastly important to the future of education and the success of our nation and the world to solve the multitude of challenges we face today."

—Carla Hannaford, Author
Smart Moves: Why Learning Is Not All in Your Head and
Playing in the Unified Field: Raising and Becoming Conscious, Creative Human Beings

"Fanatically Formative describes the process that closely parallels the remarkable transformations that we experienced at Simpson Central School upon implementation of the Early Learning Success Initiatives (e.g., use of essential skills inventories, instructional match time in literacy and numeracy, motor skills instruction, development of a positive school culture). This book is the road map that will lead to success for young learners."

—Glen Harris, Superintendent of Education, and Debbie David, Principal
Simpson County School District and Simpson Central School, Pinola, MS

"This may be the education book of the decade. Rarely does an academic work grip the reader so powerfully. Educators will come away inspired and appalled. It is my hope that Sornson's book prompts leaders in education to prioritize authentic early learning success policies that can help more children become motivated learners for life."

—Danny Brassell, Professor
California State University, Dominguez Hills

"Fanatically Formative is a compelling masterpiece that can save education as we know it. In a day and age when we are pushing students through standards at a rapid rate, yet have more students coming to us 'at risk' than ever, something has to give! Sornson offers a model for quality teaching and early intervention that can lead us to school reform that will actually make a difference."

cational Consultant and Founder
tegic Intervention Solutions, Inc.

"Fanatically Formative is fantastically informati  *o a clear vision for action. Set clear attainable learning outcomes, teach responsively,* lls, build a truly positive classroom

and school culture, collaborate to help young children succeed, include parents, and make schools filled with joy. This book makes me believe we can!"

—Derek Wheaton, Early Elementary Principal
Mattawan Consolidated School District, Mattawan, MI

"Fanatically Formative is another example of Bob Sornson's contributions to all educators who want to reach all students! The ideas are clear and compelling and, if implemented, will positively affect young children everywhere!"

—Kathy Donagrandi, Administrator
Department of Student Services, Livonia Public Schools, Livonia, MI

"With passionate conviction, Bob Sornson addresses a question we should all keep at the forefront of our discussions: How can we create schools that are responsive to students rather than driven by outside forces? Using an easy-to-read format of real-life examples, Bob challenges us to slow down and assume personal responsibility for ensuring that our students become 'good readers for life' from the earliest grades. It is my fervent hope that educators will heed Bob's call to focus on what really matters."

—Mary Howard, Author
RTI From All Sides and *Moving Forward With RTI*

"In an era of reform, Fanatically Formative teaches, reminds, and stretches what is right about education. Sornson intricately marries research with reality to make assessment and accountability relevant for all. His model is filled with heart and reminds us to not outsmart our common sense when it comes to educating, growing, and developing lifelong learners."

—Jennifer Jennings, Founder
Is It Summer Yet?! Inc.

"Fanatically Formative is an excellent guide for both teachers and administrators who can no longer bear to see more children falling behind in the rigid 'rush to cover' climate that characterizes the era of high-stakes testing. Do you want to change that climate and rediscover the craft of teaching in your school district? Sornson promises no magic tricks, but offers an inspiring model for meaningful instruction and early intervention that can actually make a difference."

—Suzanne Klein
Founder and CEO, WriteSteps

"Bob Sornson has not only successfully addressed a challenging topic in the world of educating young children, but has done so in a way that shows he understands! He understands early childhood curriculum. He understands formative assessment. He understands how to best help anyone reading this book make a difference by using a very simple, yet thorough, easily managed process."

—Lynne Ecenbarger, Education Consultant
Fort Wayne, IN

"This is it! Teachers have known for a long time the standardized testing and content expectation train is taking our students in the wrong direction. This book is the roundhouse needed to help us turn the engine and take our students through essential skills heading straight for success."

—Catherine Hernandez, Teacher
Detroit Public Schools, Detroit, MI

"The best teachers are the ones who are hungry for knowledge and are driven to make a difference for individual children. This important book merges theory and practice and provides the reader with a template for improving everyday instruction."

—Mary Johnstone, Principal
Rabbit Creek Elementary School, Anchorage, AK

"This comprehensive book—Fanatically Formative—holds the key to ensure that all students are given a rich foundation in the essential skills that will give them the foundation to be successful in school. I highly recommend Fanatically Formative to use in your district to make meaningful change. The foundation of Early Learning Success will impact the lives of students and increase student achievement in their district."

—Debra Krauss, Chief Academic Officer
Huron School District, New Boston, MI

Fanatically
FORMATIVE

Bob Sornson

Fanatically FORMATIVE

Successful Learning During the Crucial K–3 Years

CORWIN
A SAGE Company

CORWIN
A SAGE Company

FOR INFORMATION:

Corwin
A SAGE Company
2455 Teller Road
Thousand Oaks, California 91320
(800) 233-9936
www.corwin.com

SAGE Publications Ltd.
1 Oliver's Yard
55 City Road
London EC1Y 1SP
United Kingdom

SAGE Publications India Pvt. Ltd.
B 1/I 1 Mohan Cooperative Industrial Area
Mathura Road, New Delhi 110 044
India

SAGE Publications Asia-Pacific Pte. Ltd.
3 Church Street
#10–04 Samsung Hub
Singapore 049483

Acquisitions Editor: Arnis Burvikovs
Associate Editor: Desirée Bartlett
Editorial Assistant: Kimberly Greenberg
Production Editor: Amy Schroller
Copy Editor: Amy Rosenstein
Typesetter: C&M Digitals (P) Ltd.
Proofreader: Wendy Jo Dymond
Indexer: Diggs Publication Services
Cover Designer: Karine Hovsepian
Permissions Editor: Karen Ehrmann

Printed in the United States of America

A catalog record of this book is available from the Library of Congress.

ISBN 978-1-4522-2518-0

This book is printed on acid-free paper.

SUSTAINABLE FORESTRY INITIATIVE

Certified Chain of Custody
Promoting Sustainable Forestry
www.sfiprogram.org
SFI-01268

SFI label applies to text stock

12 13 14 15 16 10 9 8 7 6 5 4 3 2 1

Contents

Preface

IN MY CLASSROOM

All my students will develop the skills and behaviors they need to succeed.

Each child will get the time needed to develop the essential skills.

I will offer essential instruction at the correct instructional level.

In my class, children will feel physically and emotionally safe.

I will help children discover the importance and joy of learning.

Each day, children will experience positive relationships, respect, empathy, and love.

For decades, American schools have been engaged in a failed experiment, attempting to cram more content into a typical teaching day than humanly possible, asking children to learn overwhelming content at younger and younger ages without taking the time to build the foundation skills needed for learning success or behavioral success, and creating anxiety-filled classrooms in which children are less likely to fall deeply in love with learning. Fortunately, that is changing. There are educators across the country who understand the importance of the early childhood learning years and recognize that any school improvement initiative will have lesser results if we allow students to become compromised learners in the early years of school; these educators are beginning to stand up and speak up for good practice.

These educators are no longer willing to deliver a nonviable curriculum that attempts to cover vast amounts of content at the cost of failing to help children deeply understand and know how to use essential early learning skills. Teachers and administrators are recognizing that racing through rigidly paced or scripted lessons contributes to many students struggling and becoming disengaged from the learning process. These educators are choosing to become skilled observers of children, formatively assessing what students know and are ready to learn, and then delivering instruction well matched to the needs of their students.

For some teachers, this is a daunting challenge. Decades of pressure to cover greater and greater numbers of grade-level content objectives, indicate which objectives were "covered" in their weekly lesson plans, and keep up with the pacing guide have compromised their ability to teach to deep understanding. Decades of preparing for quarterly assessments of content covered, and preparing for state- or district-required data collection and standardized testing have reinforced one-size-fits-all instructional practices. These teachers have succumbed to the pressure to "cover" content. They have decreased attention to observing children carefully, finding their specific learning readiness levels, discovering their special interests, and understanding the background experiences that shape each student's knowledge base. Curriculum-driven instructional practices have replaced carefully designed instruction to meet the needs of their students.

In some districts, it will take an act of courage to stand up to the pressure-packed curriculum-driven juggernaut, to recognize out loud that this is harming many children and leading to poor outcomes compared with our international competition. At first, educators who speak up may feel outside the mainstream of school reform efforts that criticize teachers for not working hard enough, demand additional accountability requirements, and devise onerous teacher-evaluation systems.

It may be difficult to be the one who speaks up for slowing down the pace of instruction, for teaching less content but teaching it better, for giving some children the extra time needed to understand a concept or skill deeply, for letting children play and laugh, for abandoning a model that treats all children as if they are at the same level of readiness, for taking the time to develop language and social skills, for taking the time to build a classroom culture in which children are emotionally and physically safe, or for insisting that good early childhood classrooms are filled with joy. It may be uncomfortable to be the one who insists that we must devise a system that encourages teachers to do more than robotically deliver scripted content. But it is time for a groundswell of educators and community leaders to speak up for a system that values great teaching, attracts the best young women and men to this profession, and nurtures the development of master teachers.

Quality teaching practice is well described by research and by the experience of thoughtful educators around the world. By reading this book, you may become a fanatic for good practice and insist on using practices that help every young child develop the early learning skills and behaviors needed to become a successful lifelong learner.

Fanatically Formative offers readers both a big picture and the nitty-gritty details of school reform in the first few grades. You will understand how important the early childhood learning phase really is and how poorly many American students are doing. You will consider the long-term costs of failing to improve early learning outcomes for all of our children, and especially poor and at-risk children. Readers will better understand how an ineffective curriculum-driven system developed, how educators can support each other in the development of models of effective practice, and how to deal with some of the challenges that will come along. The importance of quality preschool and parent engagement is explored. Pathfinders whose work leads us toward exceptional practice are celebrated. Specific action plans are offered for teachers, administrators, parents, and community leaders. Readers will glimpse the train wreck that awaits us if we ignore the need for constructive change and readers will learn that we can choose a better future for our children.

This book is a call to action, an invitation for a legion of educators to become fanatically formative. Although the typical early childhood classroom may be curriculum driven, racing through content with some students who are bored and many who are overwhelmed, the fanatically formative teacher will insist on identifying essential learning outcomes and using formative assessment to have meaningful data on which to plan instruction that works for her students.

Although the typical K–3 classroom delivers the same content to all students at the same pace, the fanatically formative teacher recognizes that some children need more time and deserve more time. She optimizes learning outcomes by giving children learning activities at their instructional readiness level. She understands that pushing kids into the frustration zone causes less learning and lower test scores and does not allow herself to be bullied by well-intentioned colleagues into hurting children.

While the typical classroom is filled with teacher anxiety and student anxiety, the fanatically formative teacher takes the time to build culture. She teaches school behaviors and practices them until they become classroom routines, knowing that children learn better when social expectations are clear. She builds trust and relationship with her students, knowing that children learn better when they trust and love their teacher. She builds emotional and physical safety, knowing that many children need that safety to be able to optimally attend, learn, and remember.

While the typical classroom is pressure packed, the fanatically formative teacher has a viable curriculum based on the Common Core State Standards or state power standards, offers reteaching or additional practice to students who need it, and offers extended learning options to those who are ready. She has time for projects to integrate learning and activities to make learning come alive in her classroom.

The fanatically formative teacher recognizes that great learning is more likely to occur in a classroom in which there are engaged learners, where there is laughter, and where students support each other. The fanatically formative teacher recognizes the relationship between great teaching and joy, both for herself and for the students she serves.

We have an opportunity to choose to build great classrooms and schools in which student learning is effectively nurtured, or we can continue the pressure-packed curriculum-driven juggernaut. We can choose to build schools that develop student engagement rather than frustration and apathy. We can create schools that attract the best possible candidates to become educators, or we can continue to push teachers into dissatisfaction and failure. We can create systems that work smarter rather than always harder.

This book offers the reasons, the research, and the action steps for transforming our K–3 classrooms into kinder and more effective centers of learning. The resolution to act will come from you. Imagine the impact of schools in which teachers identify essential early learning and behavior outcomes, use formative assessment to understand what students are ready to learn, teach responsively at the student's instructional level, give extra time or help as needed, work within a safe and connected classroom and school culture, help students experience respect and empathy, rediscover the joy of teaching, and help students fall in love with learning. Imagine a generation of children educated in fanatically formative classrooms. For the future of your children and your community, stand up and speak up!

Publisher's Acknowledgments

Corwin would like to thank the following individuals for taking the time to provide their editorial insight:

Donna Adkins
Teacher
Arkadelphia Public Schools
Arkadelphia, AR

Catherine Hernandez
Teacher
Detroit Public Schools
Detroit, MI

Debra Rose Howell
Teacher
Monte Cristo Elementary
Granite Falls, WA

Sharon Jefferies
Retired Teacher
Orange County Public Schools
Orlando, FL

Mary Johnstone
Principal
Rabbit Creek Elementary School
Anchorage, AK

About the Author

Bob Sornson, PhD, was a classroom teacher and school administrator for more than 30 years and is the founder of the Early Learning Foundation. His implementation of programs and strategies for early learning success, the Early Learning Success Initiative, serves as a model for districts around the country. He is committed to the belief that practically every child can have a successful early learning experience.

Photo by Lynn Gregg.

The Early Learning Foundation is dedicated to helping schools and parents give every child an opportunity to achieve early learning success, which lays the foundation for success in life. Few things are so important to the future of our children and our society. Children who come to school without important language, literacy, numeracy, motor, and behavioral skills are at a disadvantage for success in the first years of school. Children who have not developed solid skills by the end of the third grade are at a disadvantage for life.

Dr. Sornson is the author of numerous articles, books, and audio recordings, including *Teaching and Joy* (ASCD), *Preventing Early Learning Failure* (ASCD), *Meeting the Challenge* (Love and Logic Press), *Creating Classrooms Where Teachers Love to Teach and Students Love to Learn* (Love and Logic Press), and *Number Facts and Jumping Jacks* (Crystal Springs Books). *Love and Logic on the Bus* (Love and Logic Press) is his most recent audio training program. His assessment instruments include *The Essential Skills Inventories, K–3* (Early Learning Foundation).

Dr. Sornson works with schools and education organizations across the country, focusing primarily on developing comprehensive programs that support early learning success, building classroom and school culture to support the development of social and behavioral skills, and offering parent training. He offers workshops and keynotes, and develops long-term training projects with selected organizations. Dr. Sornson can be contacted at **earlylearningfoundation.com.**

Students at Risk   1

It was already the second week of school when Tyrel came into class for the first time. It was getting close to lunchtime when his father brought him to be registered as a student. The principal walked Tyrel to the first-grade classroom as soon as the paperwork was completed. The young boy stood uncomfortably at the door to Mrs. Peterson's classroom for a moment, until she took him by the hand and led him to a seat at a table.

He was dressed in a faded T-shirt and pants that were too long for him, Mrs. Peterson noted. He dropped his backpack on the floor and slouched in the chair.

"Jimmy," she asked quietly, "Would you show Tyrel our class routine for hanging up coats and putting away backpacks please?"

She watched as the two boys walked together to the back of the classroom. The other students were finishing a math assignment and beginning to clear their tables in preparation for lunch. Mrs. Peterson surveyed her classroom. Susie was bossing Ralph again, telling him to hurry up with his work so they wouldn't be late for lunch. He tried to ignore her, but she persisted. Junie and Jessica had forgotten about their math and somehow wandered over to the art center. How had she failed to notice them? Mrs. Peterson smiled to herself. Abigail and Kendra were finished putting away their work and had started to crawl under the table. Reflecting on the many classroom procedures that still needed practice, she called the children to attention and told them she'd be calling on them to line up for lunch by table as soon as everything was put away.

This was already a much practiced procedure, and most of the students began getting ready. There was a tug on her pants. Looking down, it was Jimmy, standing next to Tyrel.

"He doesn't have any lunch, or any lunch money," Jimmy informed her while pointing at Tyrel.

She bent down to their level. "That is not a problem. I'll make sure Tyrel gets lunch," responded Mrs. Peterson, looking at both boys. "Jimmy, would you show Tyrel how we stand in line and tell him all about going to the lunchroom? You can help him go through the hot-lunch line today."

Tyrel was looking away, looking at the floor. The teacher reached out and touched his shoulder. "We'll take good care of you here," she assured him.

He looked up at her. "I got no money. I'm sorry I got no money."

"That's all right. Do you like chicken?"

He nodded.

"Good. I think we have chicken today. Do you like corn?"

Tyrel nodded.

"Good. I think we have corn today. Do you like ice cream?"

This time he nodded vigorously.

"Good. I think we have ice cream today. Do you like spinach?"

He gave her a quizzical look. It made her laugh. "I really like spinach, but they never seem to have it in the lunchroom. I wonder why," she mused aloud. "I have some wonderful spinach growing in my garden at home. I will try to remember to bring some for you boys very soon. It'll be a special treat," she told them with a look of anticipation.

With 25 years of experience as an elementary teacher, Mrs. Peterson watched her classroom with an experienced eye. Many of her children had limited oral language skills and struggled to express themselves and to understand any complex classroom instructions. It was easier to count the children with appropriate social skills than the ones who struggled with social behaviors. Several were physically awkward as they moved about the room and struggled to hold a pencil or scissors correctly. Most of these also had poor hand strength. Even though this was first grade, she had already determined that nine of her students did not yet know all of the basic letter sounds, and three could not yet name all the letters. She wondered about Tyrel, her new student. It seemed likely there were gaps in his readiness for the demands of school.

She watched him as the class walked in a wandering line toward the cafeteria. He was staying close to Jimmy, carefully watching his new friend for clues about living in this new school. Already she felt the connection with him. Mrs. Peterson knew Tyrel would need lots of extra help this year, and she also knew that the children who take the most work are often the one's we remember so clearly for years. But this year, there were more children who needed extra help than she could ever remember. It was a trend, she reminded herself. Some days she wondered if she were a magnet for these needy ones.

Maybe I am, she wondered. That wouldn't be so bad.

It's true. There are more children at risk of struggling to be successful in the early years of school. Preschool and primary level teachers widely observe more children with language delays, gross motor skill delays, visual-motor skill delays, and behavioral and social skills that make learning difficult. These at-risk students are coming to school at a time when learning success has never been so important. Although there was a time when teenagers with limited academic skills could quit school and find decent-paying work on farms or in factories, those days are long gone. The learning society and the information age are here, and so are these greater numbers of needy children.

For a moment Mrs. Peterson felt the weight of it. Looking at her line of beautifully imperfect children, she saw the importance of helping each one find the learning success needed for ongoing academic and social learning success and for success in life.

The early childhood years are the most important learning phase in the life of a child. During these years, the brain is growing and developing complexity at greater rates than in any other phase of life. The trajectory of learning success is clearly established during these years. Children who have significant gaps in essential early learning skills by the end of third grade are at a disadvantage for life (President's Commission on Excellence in Special Education, 2002).

The research is unequivocal. Children who experience reading success in the early years are more likely to become good readers for life (Alexander & Entwisle, 1988; Snow, Burns, & Griffin, 1998; Torgesen, 1998; Tuscano, 1999; Vellutino, Scanlon, & Tanzman, 1998). Children who do not experience early learning success are more likely to drop out and are more likely to engage in substance abuse and other risky behaviors (Barnett, 1996; Blum, Beuhring, & Rinehart, 2000; Currie & Duncan, 1995). In an extensive study of students in the San Diego Public Schools (Zau & Betts, 2008), it was demonstrated that students at risk of failing the California state-required high school exit exam (administered in 10th grade) can be identified almost as well in fourth grade as they can in ninth grade. The San Diego study highlights the inefficiency of waiting until high school to help students who are at risk of learning failure when we have known for years who they are and in which areas of learning they are at risk.

In 2007, nearly 6.2 million young Americans (16% of the 16–24 age group) were high school dropouts (Northeastern University, Center for Labor Market Studies and Alternative Schools Network in Chicago, 2009). Every student who does not complete high school costs our society an estimated $260,000 in lost earnings, taxes, and productivity (Riley & Peterson, 2008). But most parents know that high school graduation is not enough in the information society. High school graduation is not sufficient to find entry into the higher-paying jobs in today's economy. We want our children to have solid learning skills, a love of learning, and be ready to continue to train and retrain throughout their professional lifetimes.

According to a special report from the Annie E. Casey Foundation (2010), 67% of American children are scoring below proficient reading levels at the beginning of fourth grade on the National Assessment of Educational Progress reading test. Of these, 34% read at the *basic* level and 33% read at the *below basic* level. One in six children who are not reading proficiently in third grade fail to graduate from high school on time, four times the rate for children with proficient third-grade reading skills. "These scores are profoundly disappointing to all of us who see school success and high school graduation as beacons in the battle against intergenerational poverty" (Annie E. Casey Foundation, 2010, p. 2).

Three quarters of students who are poor readers in third grade will remain poor readers in high school (U.S. Department of Education, 1999). Students with poor literacy skills are more likely to have behavioral and social problems in subsequent grades (Miles & Stipek, 2006). The National Research Council (1998) asserts that "academic success, as defined by high school graduation, can be predicted with reasonable accuracy by knowing someone's reading skill at the end of third grade. A person who is not at least a modestly skilled reader by that time is unlikely to graduate from high school."

> Sixty-seven percent of American children are scoring below proficient reading levels at the beginning of fourth grade on the National Assessment of Educational Progress reading test.
>
> Annie E. Casey Foundation (2010)

For poor children the story is even worse. Overall, 22% of children who have lived in poverty (for at least 1 year) do not graduate from high school on time, compared with 6% of those who have never been poor. For children who have lived more than half of their childhood in poverty, this rate rises to 32% (Hernandez, 2011). This rate is 16 times greater than the 2% dropout rate among proficient readers who have never been poor.

Nationwide, 55% of fourth graders in moderate- and high-income families have reading skills below the proficient level. This increases to 83%

for children in low-income families (Hernandez, 2011). For Latino, Black, and American Indian children, the numbers are staggering. More than 80% cannot read at grade level by fourth grade. If children do not gain the skills and habits necessary to succeed in school by age 8, they are more likely to struggle to perform well and be less motivated for future learning in middle school and high school. They will also struggle to develop the higher-order thinking, communication, analytic, and social skills that are the essential for success in life (Foundation for Child Development, 2011).

Entering the cafeteria that day with her class, Mrs. Peterson saw Jimmy take Tyrel's hand. Months later she could look back and identify that moment of transformation. In that instant she considered her beautiful but needy students as they filed into the cafeteria. She saw some with delayed language skills, awkward motor skills, and lack of social awareness, but she also saw the hopefulness in the eyes of these children. She saw their capacity for trust, their openness to learning, their hunger to live full lives. Mrs. Peterson considered the pressures of her school system, including the overwhelming

> Eighty-three percent of fourth graders from poor families have reading skills below the proficient level.
>
> Hernandez (2011)
>
> Three quarters of students who are poor readers in third grade will remain poor readers in high school.
>
> Shaywitz et al. (1997)

content expectations, paperwork requirements, overcrowding, understaffing, the constant din of new program requirements, and the educational fad of the month. When she saw Jimmy take Tyrel's hand that day, something changed inside of her. She found a resolve and a sense of peace.

I won't let them fail. They will not leave my class without the skills they need, she promised.

Whatever it takes, she thought. *I've been teaching for 25 years, and I'd like another good 10 years. I can do this. I'm going to focus on giving these kids every skill they need to be successful learners throughout their lives. I will reject the pressure to cover material they don't understand. I will figure out what's most important, and teach each child at his or her level of readiness. My students will fall in love with learning. I'll get help, somehow. Tyrel and Jimmy, Junie and Jessica, Susie and Ralph, Abigail and Kendra, and all the rest of these students will get what they need to succeed. These beautiful children will not become part of the grim statistics. All my students will develop the skills and behaviors they need to succeed. No excuses.*

Across the busy cafeteria she could hear Junie calling her for help. Mrs. Peterson felt it deep within herself. She wondered how she would ever keep this promise.

CHAPTER 1 STUDY QUESTIONS

1. Why are we seeing more children at risk of early learning failure coming to our school?

2. Does our district recognize the importance of proficient skills by the end of third grade?

3. How could we recognize children who are struggling even earlier than third grade?

4. The research clearly establishes the importance of literacy by the end of third grade. Do numeracy skills also need to be well established in the early grades? What about patterns of behavior that are established in this same time frame?

5. Children who are not proficient readers and also live in poverty are far more at risk of falling into patterns of failure. What can we do about this in our schools and community?

Responsive Instruction Versus Curriculum-Driven Instruction

2

Why Public Education's Race to Cover More Material and Test More Students Is Failing America's Children

As she passed out the math worksheets, Mrs. Peterson glanced thoughtfully at Tyrel. She had not yet had a chance to assess his skills, and she wondered how he would manage the assignment. Following the math program guidelines, she did a brief demonstration of the addition problem on the whiteboard. She asked Suzie to help her model another problem, but she knew she was no longer following the prescribed lesson. Then she handed out the worksheets. Every child received the same worksheet. She paused as she handed the page to those children who might not be ready.

"This is easy," pronounced Sarah.

"Yes, Sarah," responded Mrs. Peterson. "When you are done you can go to the math center." The math center was another one of Mrs. Peterson's adaptations to the standard lesson plans.

Several children hurried to work. Jimmy and Abigail studied the numbers on their worksheet. Kendra raised her hand and asked Mrs. Peterson for help. Moving among students who were asking for help, the teacher noticed Tyrel sitting quietly. His pencil was on the floor.

"How are you doing, Tyrel?" she asked quietly moving next to him.

He shrugged and looked away.

Kneeling beside him, she asked, "Have you done problems like this before?"

"Sure," Tyrel nodded.

"Let's work together for a minute. What is this problem here?"

Tyrel fidgeted in his seat.

"What is this first number?"

"Seven," Tyrel answered correctly.

"And how many do you add to seven?" asked Mrs. Peterson pointing to the second number.

"That's four."

"So seven plus four gives you . . ."

"Ten?"

Reaching into her pocket, Mrs. Peterson brought out a handful of coins. She placed seven on the table in front of Tyrel. "How many is this?"

Carefully he studied his teacher's face. Seeing no frustration there, he looked down at the coins.

"How many are here, Tyrel?"

Tyrel reached out his finger and counted seven.

"Nice. Now how many are here?" she said after putting four more pennies on the table in a separate group.

Again he counted with his finger. "Four?"

"Perfect answer. And now, how many do we have altogether?"

Tyrel looked puzzled.

"Let's count all the pennies." With her help, Tyrel finger-counted all the pennies.

"Eleven?" he said, tentatively.

"Perfect again!" exclaimed Mrs. Peterson.

Sweeping aside the worksheet, Mrs. Peterson practiced counting pennies with Tyrel. Within a few minutes, he could correctly finger-count any number to 12 but sometimes got lost and miscounted numbers between 13 and 20.

Junie was standing next to Mrs. Peterson, tugging gently on her sleeve for attention. Asking Junie to wait for just another moment, the teacher found a preschool-level counting worksheet for Tyrel and showed him how to begin.

At home that evening, Mrs. Peterson settled into her chair. It was the Thursday night ritual. Lesson plans for the following week were due tomorrow, and teachers were expected to show which grade-level content expectations would be included in that week's lessons. By the end of the year, all of the nearly 300 state grade-level content expectations were to be covered, according to a district directive several years back. She shifted uncomfortably in her chair. Mrs. Peterson had devised a good plan for next week, including small groups, whole group instruction, center activities, and individualized reading time with parent volunteers. Now she tried to fit in the codes for the grade-level content expectations. It just didn't fit with her understanding of a good lesson plan.

For Mrs. Peterson, a good plan included activities and content that kept students learning at just the right level of challenge for as much of the school day as possible. Because her students were at such different levels, writing a plan that implied she had "covered" one of the Grade Level Content Expectations (GLCEs) was preposterous. If she tried to "cover" GLCE 1.G.4.1: *Use combinations of shapes to make a new shape to demonstrate relationships between shapes (e.g., a hexagon can be made from six triangles)*, it might be a good instructional match for Sarah and Phillip, but Tyrel, Junie, and Jessica would be completely lost. They didn't yet have one-to-one correspondence for counting numbers to 20.

It was a farce in which Mrs. Peterson had participated for years. When teachers were first asked to write GLCE references in their lesson plans, they met for months and earnestly tried to find a way to cover all of the content expectations within the school year. They tried to squeeze more into the curriculum, encouraging each other to believe that covering more might actually be possible. But eventually it became clear they could not measure up to what they perceived to be the state's expectations. Some of the GLCEs seemed developmentally mismatched to the readiness of their students. Other content expectations were so obtuse that they defied understanding. Eventually, with heavy hearts, the grade-level teams of teachers divided each content area into units, ascribed GLCEs to each unit, and turned in the written plan to cover all the expectations. Cover, introduce, allude to, or mention hastily in passing, it had all become a race that no teacher could ever win.

Somehow good teaching had become correlated to covering more content. The conversation shifted. What unit are you on? Is your class ahead of mine? Am I teaching too slowly? Are my students more challenged than yours? Did you finish the textbook this year? More is better. Faster is better. It's the law, some teachers began to say. We are required to cover the content expectations with all students. Teach more, teach faster, teach harder.

> **Teach more; teach faster; teach harder.**

"Matthew," called Mrs. Peterson, "I need your help."

Her teenaged son answered from upstairs. "I am kind of busy."

"Come down anyway," she replied. "I need some help with a Google search."

He bumped down the stairs. "You know how to do a search."

She smiled at her big son. "I do, but you are so much faster than me at finding the information I need."

They searched *viable content first grade,* and *early learning success.* Matthew found several relevant sites and articles, and then trudged back to his homework.

Viable content is the content that can actually be addressed in the time available (Marzano, 2003). American schools have been increasing content expectations over the last few decades, asking teachers to cover more content even as more students come to school with significant learning delays. Forty-six percent of U.S. kindergartners come to school at risk for failure (U.S. Department of Education, 2001). But the push to ask teachers to cover more continues.

In the 1980s and 1990s, organizations advocating the importance of science, math, history, geography, civics, literature, core knowledge, writing, art, music, anthropology, political science, personal hygiene, sex education, self-help skills, personal finance, and other important aspects of human knowledge issued lengthy recommendations regarding the importance of their subject and lists of topics that "should" be covered in our schools. Pundits and comics deplored the state of ignorance displayed by the man-on-the-street interviews of many Americans. In 2011, when *Newsweek* asked 1,000 U.S. citizens to take America's official citizenship test, 29% couldn't name the vice president, 73% couldn't correctly say why we fought the Cold War, 44% were unable to define the Bill of Rights, and 6% could not circle Independence Day on a calendar (Romano, 2011). In a survey conducted by the U.S. Mint, only 7% of those surveyed could name the first four presidents in order: George Washington, John Adams, Thomas Jefferson, and James Madison (U.S. Mint, 2007).

It is easy to understand the clamor for more knowledge. It is easy to understand how citizens and decision makers look to the school for answers. But racing through more content is not working, and it is time to look more thoughtfully for solutions.

Schmoker and Marzano (1999) advise educators, "We will realize the promise of school reform when we establish standards and expectations for reaching them that are clear, not confusing; essential, not exhaustive. The result will be a new coherence and a shared focus that could be the most propitious step we can take toward educating all students well" (p. 17).

Mrs. Peterson had made a promise to herself; *All my students will develop the skills and behaviors they need to succeed.* Trying to cover *more, faster, sooner* was failing many of her students, especially those most vulnerable. She began to consider different solutions.

Sometimes you cannot find good answers because you have not asked the right questions. With the perspective that comes with 25 years of experience working with young children, Mrs. Peterson considered different questions. Which skills and behaviors are most important? Which skills last? Which skills are likely to support academic success in other academic subjects? Which skills support social learning? Which skills are essential building blocks for higher-level learning? What instructional practices help students be more engaged, spend more time on task, learn more, and behave better? How do I give my students more time learning the skills they need most at the correct level of challenge?

In the race to be ready for mandated state testing, most schools have adopted a curriculum-driven approach to learning. Teachers are given a set of materials, content expectations, pacing guides, district assessments, and in some cases scripted teaching materials and then asked to cover all aspects of the impossibly ambitious curriculum. The emphasis is on getting the material covered. But 67% of American children are scoring below proficient reading levels at the beginning of fourth grade, the point at which we can predict long-term learning success for proficient learners (Annie E. Casey Foundation, 2010), and 61% of American children are scoring below proficient levels at the beginning of fourth grade in math (National Assessment of Educational Progress [NEAP], 2009).

This curriculum-driven approach works in conflict with one of the most time-tested tenets of good teaching, that children learn more when they work at the correct level of challenge. Vygotsky (1978, 1986) called this the "zone of proximal development" when describing optimal learning

> If you wanted to teach all of the standards in the national documents, you would have to change schooling from K–12 to K–22.
>
> - 255 standards across 14 subject areas
> - 3,500 benchmarks
> - 13,000 hours of class time available
> - 9,000 hours of instruction available
> - 15,500 hours of instruction needed to cover the 3,500 benchmarks
>
> Robert Marzano (2006)

Too much content

Poor instructional match

situations for young children and encouraged educators and parents to present tasks at slight levels of challenge, then tiered learning activities leading toward higher levels of functioning. Betts (1946) tried to quantify the degree of challenge associated with independent, instructional, and frustration levels of reading. His work was followed by Gickling and Armstrong (1978), who supported the basic categorization of levels. Gickling went on to demonstrate the relationship between instructional level and on-task behaviors, task completion, and comprehension (Gickling & Armstrong, 1978; Gickling & Rosenfield, 1995). Fuchs and colleagues (2006) expanded the application of instructional match to mathematics and other types of learning.

In the development of Reading Recovery, a first-grade reading intervention program, Marie Clay used practice reading at the appropriate instructional level as one of the foundations of successful early reading practice (Clay, 1993, 1998; Pinnell, 1989). The importance of design of instruction at the correct level of challenge is well accepted. Allington (2001), Jensen (2005), Marzano (2003, 2007), Marzano, Pickering, and Pollock (2001), Sornson (2001), Torgesen (2002), Ysseldyke and colleagues (1987), and others include instructional match as a necessary factor for good instruction. Simply put, teaching students at their instructional level improves learning outcomes. Pushing students into their frustration zone slows learning, reduces motivation, reduces time on-task, and increases the likelihood of behavior problems.

Teachers differentiate instruction to give students learning time at the correct level of challenge and in areas of personal interest. Leveled reading, guided reading, and Readers' Workshop offer students practice at

Teaching Children to Read	
Frustration Level	Less than 93% sight-word recognition accuracy
Instructional Level	93% to 97% accuracy (optimal learning range)
Independent Level	98% to 100% sight-word recognition accuracy
Gickling and Armstrong (1978)	

the correct instructional level. Learning centers and plan-do-review help students learn to pick instructional activities that are a good match for readiness. Quality computer-assisted instruction matches instruction to learner success to optimize rates of learning.

Curriculum-driven instruction focuses on covering impossibly large lists of content expectations. *By taking responsibility for material selection and individual student pacing away from the classroom teacher,* curriculum-driven instruction minimizes or nullifies opportunities for teachers to carefully match instruction to the specific needs of students. Curriculum-driven instruction (too much, too fast, same for all) contributes to our poor outcomes and is contrary to best practice in higher-performing educational systems around the world. In countries with the highest achievement, fewer topics are covered each year, but they are covered in greater depth (National Council of Teachers of Mathematics, 2005, 2006; National Mathematics Advisory Council, 2008).

The Organisation for Economic Co-operation and Development (OECD) Programme for International Student Assessment (PISA) report, published every 3 years, which compares the knowledge and skills of 15-year-olds, ranked the United States 14th out of 34 OECD countries for reading skills, 17th for science, and a below-average 25th for mathematics (OECD, 2010). American students did not rank among the top-10 performers in any category.

Math rankings PISA, 2010	Science rankings PISA, 2010	Reading rankings PISA, 2010
1. Shanghai-China	1. Shanghai-China	1. Shanghai-China
2. Singapore	2. Finland	2. Korea
3. Hong Kong-China	3. Hong Kong-China	3. Finland
4. Korea	4. Singapore	4. Hong Kong-China
5. Chinese Taipei	5. Japan	5. Singapore
6. Finland	6. Korea	6. Canada
7. Liechtenstein	7. New Zealand	7. New Zealand
8. Switzerland	8. Canada	8. Japan
9. Japan	9. Estonia	9. Australia
10. Canada	10. Australia	10. Netherlands

The National Council of Teachers of Mathematics recommends that math curriculum should include fewer topics, spending enough time to make sure each is learned in enough depth that it need not be revisited in later grades. That is the approach used in most top-performing nations.

National Mathematics
Advisory Council (2008)

Having decided that she would no longer be pushed to offer too much, too fast, and same-for-all instruction, Mrs. Peterson began working on a list of principles that would guide her to plan instruction that is responsive to the specific needs of her students.

All my students will develop the skills and behaviors they need to succeed.

Not only were there way too many grade-level content expectations to teach or monitor progress toward successful completion, but there were also important aspects of development not described in the GLCEs.

More of Mrs. Peterson's students were coming to school with significant delays in oral language skills, including receptive and expressive language, and vocabulary. This was especially true for children living in poverty. Oral language is directly related to readiness for literacy, numeracy, and social skill success. While racing through curriculum-driven instructional programs, there was not enough time to help children learn to develop these oral language skills.

Many of her students, especially in recent years, had significant delays in the development of basic motor skills. Some moved awkwardly, struggled with balance, could not skip, held a pencil poorly, and could not hold and use a scissors. More students struggled with basic visual-motor skills and tended to avoid activities that required sustained use of hand-eye skills.

Basic phonologic skills were an area of weakness for some. These children often had difficulty listening, failed to recognize rhyming words and sound patterns, and struggled to learn letter sounds. Some children did not have basic numeracy skills required for the first-grade math curriculum. They had difficulty counting, did not have one-to-one correspondence, and could not recognize the value of a group of dots on dice or dominoes.

And many of Mrs. Peterson's children struggled with basic social skills and school behaviors. Helping her students learn basic classroom routines, learn to play well with each other, and learn empathy and emotional control would be an important part of building the essential skills needed for success.

Each child will get the time needed to develop the essential skills.

Same-for-all instruction just does not account for the fact that there are skills that Sarah and Phillip will learn in a few minutes while Junie and Jessica might need more time. Experience, vocabulary, environment, and other individual differences will affect the time needed to develop essential outcomes. If Junie needs more time to build number skills, she will get it, promised Mrs. Peterson. If Ralph needs practice learning to balance and skip, he will get that practice until his skills are solid. If Tyrel needs more time to develop vocabulary skills, somehow they will find the time.

**I will offer essential instruction
at the correct instructional level.**

Mrs. Peterson reflected on the many times she had delivered instruction to students who were not yet ready. She could picture that faraway look or the look of fear that some children had when the work was too difficult. She could picture the boredom that some children experienced when the work was too easy. For many years now, she had carefully included an assessment of instructional readiness into her plans for teaching reading. Every good reading teacher strives to give young children reading practice at the right level of difficulty. Now she resolved to be more aware of instructional match as she taught school behaviors and routines, basic numeracy skills, basic motor skills, and every skill essential to the long-term success of her students. Pushing children to work in the frustration zone is malpractice. It diminishes their rate of learning, and it causes many children to lose the love of learning so important to becoming a lifelong learner.

In my class, children will feel physically and emotionally safe.

In some classrooms, partly because of the overwhelming content expectations, teachers have failed to take the time needed to carefully develop classroom procedures, build positive relationships with their students, and build a culture of safety and support among the students. With more children coming to school with poor social skills and standards of behavior, it is especially important that teachers help children develop these skills. Mrs. Peterson resolved to manage behavior without anger, to carefully teach and practice classroom behaviors and procedures, and to build strong social bonds with her students and their parents.

**I will help children discover
the importance and joy of learning.**

Children learn more when they see the importance of learning. Children learn more when they are motivated by the expectation of success. Children learn more when they have clear learning goals. Mrs. Peterson resolved to help children experience success in her classroom; make choices to learn about things that interest them; believe in their capacity to be successful learners; find personal meaning in reading, math, and positive social behaviors; and to find the joy in learning that can inspire them to choose to be learners for life.

Each day, children will experience positive relationships, respect, empathy, and love.

It is not on the state's list of grade-level content expectations but still it is so important. Mrs. Peterson resolved that each day her students will have a positive emotional experience. Each day they will feel respect, empathy, and love. The teacher will not just tell them to behave, but will also model courtesy and kindness. Each day they will know that the classroom is a safe place where they will find love, clear standards for good behavior, and a chance to learn important things that make their lives richer.

IN MY CLASSROOM

All my students will develop the skills and behaviors they need to succeed.

Each child will get the time needed to develop the essential skills.

I will offer essential instruction at the correct instructional level.

In my class children will feel physically and emotionally safe.

I will help children discover the importance and joy of learning.

Each day children will experience positive relationships, respect, empathy, and love.

CHAPTER 2 STUDY QUESTIONS

1. Are the grade-level content expectations in our state reasonable or are there way too many?

2. Does our state publish "power standards," those standards that are essential for the next level of learning?

3. Does our district recognize that some content objectives are more important than others?

4. Countries with more successful educational systems emphasize less content and deeper understanding of that content. Why?

5. Which of the six commitments Mrs. Peterson developed for her classroom have you already made?

6. Are Mrs. Peterson's six commitments correlated in the research to improved learning outcomes?

7. Do you consider your classroom primarily curriculum driven or responsive to the needs of individual children?

Finding Focus 3

By lunchtime, Mrs. Peterson was about done trying to be responsive to the individual needs of her students. During morning meeting, she tried to keep track of the oral language needs of children but couldn't take notes fast enough to have any meaningful data. Just trying to write down all the individual differences distracted her from carefully observing the needs of her students, and she failed to notice that Samantha was starting to weep when Marcus told about his sister who'd been sick since last week. Mrs. Peterson just could not find the right balance between recording information and staying in tune with her class. Math was a disaster. She kept running around trying to assess skills and give each child activities that were within their instructional or independent levels, but Suzie was whining that her work was too easy, and then Jason decided to switch work with Joel, and before long it was just a mess of a lesson. By lunch Mrs. Peterson was exhausted.

"I'm trying to do too much, again," she complained at lunch to her friend Mrs. Samuels.

"I thought you were learning to focus this year," teased Mrs. Samuels. She had known Mrs. Peterson for many years. They had shared trials and successes for decades.

"It's not working. My students are all so amazingly different. I keep trying to figure out how to keep them working at the right instructional level, but they are all so different. Abigail is smart, but she doesn't have any number sense yet. And Jason has number sense, but his language skills get in the way. Marcus could do anything if I could just get him to sit still."

"Did anything work well this morning?" Mrs. Samuels asked.

"Literacy time was pretty good," answered Mrs. Peterson.

"That's because you are already so skilled in teaching reading, and you know how to set it up. You've taught me guided reading, Writer's Workshop, Daily 5, running records, and practically everything else I know about teaching reading."

"But these kids need more. I may be teaching great reading lessons, but sometimes I don't know who is really learning. And I don't know why. If Jimmy isn't learning an important skill, I need to understand better what's holding him back. Is there a language delay? Or a missing phonologic skill? Is there an important motor skill that might help him sit, listen, and focus? And what about behavior and social skills? I think Joel could be a genius if I could just get him on my side."

"You can't keep track of all this," commiserated Mrs. Samuels. "You just use your intuition."

"My intuition says I could do a lot better. The district says I'm accountable for the content I cover, but has never asked me to carefully keep track of what my students learn. I know Tyrel has gaps that are holding him back, but I can't pinpoint them and if I don't soon I know he'll slide by without really getting to the solid skills he needs," declared Mrs. Peterson.

"Maybe you could just take it a little slower. Maybe you could break down the skills you want to ensure your students develop, but just take one skill area at a time."

"You're probably right. I'm making myself crabby."

"Maybe you could give yourself a learning goal that's manageable. Then you'd be giving yourself the benefit of a higher rate of success like you keep preaching we should give our students," said the experienced second-grade teacher with a smirk. "Where would you start?" she asked sweetly.

"It makes sense to start with literacy, because that's probably what we understand best," replied Mrs. Peterson slowly. "But I think I'm going to need your help," she said looking at her friend.

"Uh-oh. What am I getting myself into?"

"Let's start with an outcome analysis. You teach second grade, and you've seen hundreds of kids as they begin second grade. What are the literacy skills they absolutely positively must have to be ready for second-grade instruction?"

> We will realize the promise of school reform when we establish standards and expectations for reaching them that are clear, not confusing; essential, not exhaustive. The result will be a new coherence and a shared focus that could be the most propitious step we can take toward educating all students well.
>
> Schmoker and Marzano (1999)

The question startled them both. After years of reviewing long lists of expected outcomes, they were taking a different view. After years of scribbling Grade Level Content Expectation (GLCE) notations into lesson plans, they had discovered a far more interesting question: If they carefully assess what students know and can do, what are the skills that must be deeply learned, and available to be easily used, to ensure ongoing learning success?

The search for vital skills and behaviors that predict outcomes is not unique to education. In business, organizational leaders search for specific behaviors or skills that are associated with a desired outcome. Rather than focus on *improving collaboration*, these leaders may teach members of the team to use more positive, other-focused, and inquiry statements rather than negative and judgmental statements with fellow team members. Rather than focusing on *being more innovative*, effective change leaders may schedule time away from typical routines and expect team members to add ideas to another team member's favorite project as a way of increasing specific behaviors that drive big outcomes. Patterson, Grenny, Maxfield, McMillan, and Switzler (2008) call these vital behaviors and look carefully for the factors that create a cascade of positive change.

The identification and analysis of essential skills and behaviors in business may be most identified with the father of quality improvement, W. Edwards Deming (1982, 1986, 1993). His Fourteen Points have served as a guide for quality initiatives since he became known for his success helping Japanese businesses recover after World War II. From among his Fourteen Points, several ideas emerge that are important as we consider systems improvements that advance early learning success:

- *Instead of leaving the problems for someone else down the line, we must be proactive by quickly and effectively identifying problems and effectively intervening.*
- *Continuously improve the system by measuring key factors impacting quality learning outcomes, analyzing data regarding those factors, and then adjusting to improve learning outcomes. Deming popularized the Plan-Do-Study-Act (PDSA) cycle developed by Walter A. Shewhart.*
- *Drive out fear. Create a fear-free environment where everyone can contribute and work effectively.*
- *Break down barriers between areas. People should work cooperatively with mutual trust, respect, and appreciation for the needs of others in their work. Organizational culture is key to positive results.*
- *Most problems are system related. Deming believed that people want to do work right. It is the system that 80% to 90% of the time prevents people from doing quality work.*
- *Goals set arbitrarily, especially if they are not accompanied by feasible courses of action, have a demoralizing effect.*

- *Support ongoing and continuous education and professional skill development within the entire organization.*

Whether in corporations or schools, it should be clear that if we try to cover vastly more content than can be well taught, we dilute the effectiveness of instruction and deny the opportunity for quality learning. It is also clear that if we collect massive amounts of data regarding student learning outcomes using summative assessment tools, we may be data rich but information poor.

DRIP

Data Rich but Information Poor

Mrs. Peterson and Mrs. Samuels had begun the important process of clarifying vital factors. What are the most important skills, content and behaviors to teach? What are the most important factors to consistently measure so that instruction can be quickly adjusted if it is poorly matched to student readiness? What skills and behaviors must we ensure each student has learned to a level of deep understanding and application?

Too Much, Too Soon, Too Fast

The next few days were a pilgrimage of frustration for the veteran teachers. Mrs. Samuels brought the entire set of state grade-level content expectations for first and second grade to lunch. As they knew it would be, culling through these cumbersome documents and trying to discern the vital factors for instruction or data collection was unmanageable. Mrs. Peterson and Mrs. Samuels lapsed into a gloomy reverie over their salads.

After abandoning the GLCEs as a reasonable set of instructional goals or assessment factors, they shifted focus to a careful examination of the Common Core State Standards (CCSS) and state power standards. In most states, there are "power standards," often mentioned as the standards from which most of the state's standardized achievement test questions are derived. More importantly, they can serve as a guide to a more reasonable focus for instruction.

Power standards typically meet three criteria (Ainsworth, 2003):

1. They have leverage. Success in a power standard is likely to yield success in other academic subjects. Reading with comprehension is one of the clearest examples of a standard with leverage. Students with proficient reading skills are likely to score well in other academic subjects.

2. Power standards endure. Students who grasp a power standard will gain knowledge and skills that they can use for years, rather than knowledge with value that diminishes within minutes of the conclusion of a state test.

3. Power standards are essential for the next level of learning. If you ask teachers, "What will you give up from your curriculum?" the answer might be, "Nothing. It's all important." But, if you were to ask teachers what knowledge and skills students from the previous grade would be required to have in order to enter her class prepared and ready to learn, the teacher would probably give a succinct list of knowledge and skills that students should have.

The search for power standards was assigned to Mrs. Samuels. Known for her determination, she nonetheless could not find these standards from any state website. Fortunately, one of the young third-grade teachers overheard their conversation and directed her to a different site where the standards were finally found.

Mrs. Peterson took the lead on the study of the CCSS. Her state had agreed to move toward implementation of these as part of their application for federal funds, and with the help of her son she was easily able to find them. The CCSS were developed in a process coordinated by the National Governors Association Center for Best Practices and the Council of Chief State School Officers. They aspire to provide focus and coherence to the progression of skills across grades and are benchmarked against international outcome expectations. This supports one of the goals of the standards, which is to prepare students for the global economy.

These were a much more focused set of learning outcomes than the state GLCEs, but they presented a challenge. There were still so many. And many were unclear as to what proficiency might look like. In just the area of first-grade literacy, Mrs. Peterson found (Common Core State Standards Initiative, 2011):

FIRST-GRADE LITERACY/COMMON CORE STATE STANDARDS

Literature

Key Ideas and Details

- RL.1.1. Ask and answer questions about key details in a text.
- RL.1.2. Retell stories, including key details, and demonstrate understanding of their central message or lesson.
- RL.1.3. Describe characters, settings, and major events in a story, using key details.

Craft and Structure

- RL.1.4. Identify words and phrases in stories or poems that suggest feelings or appeal to the senses.
- RL.1.5. Explain major differences between books that tell stories and books that give information, drawing on a wide reading of a range of text types.
- RL.1.6. Identify who is telling the story at various points in a text.

Integration of Knowledge and Ideas

- RL.1.7. Use illustrations and details in a story to describe its characters, setting, or events.
- RL.1.8. (Not applicable to literature)
- RL.1.9. Compare and contrast the adventures and experiences of characters in stories.

Range of Reading and Level of Text Complexity

- RL.1.10. With prompting and support, read prose and poetry of appropriate complexity for Grade 1.

Reading: Informational Text

Key Ideas and Details

- RI.1.1. Ask and answer questions about key details in a text.
- RI.1.2. Identify the main topic and retell key details of a text.
- RI.1.3. Describe the connection between two individuals, events, ideas, or pieces of information in a text.

Craft and Structure

- RI.1.4. Ask and answer questions to help determine or clarify the meaning of words and phrases in a text.
- RI.1.5. Know and use various text features (e.g., headings, tables of contents, glossaries, electronic menus, icons) to locate key facts or information in a text.

- RI.1.6. Distinguish between information provided by pictures or other illustrations and information provided by the words in a text.

Integration of Knowledge and Ideas

- RI.1.7. Use the illustrations and details in a text to describe its key ideas.
- RI.1.8. Identify the reasons an author gives to support points in a text.
- RI.1.9. Identify basic similarities in and differences between two texts on the same topic (e.g., in illustrations, descriptions, or procedures).

Range of Reading and Level of Text Complexity

- RI.1.10. With prompting and support, read informational texts appropriately complex for grade.

Reading: Foundational Skills

Print Concepts

- RF.1.1. Demonstrate understanding of the organization and basic features of print.
  - Recognize the distinguishing features of a sentence (e.g., first word, capitalization, ending punctuation).

Phonological Awareness

- RF.1.2. Demonstrate understanding of spoken words, syllables, and sounds (phonemes).
  - Distinguish long from short vowel sounds in spoken single-syllable words.
  - Orally produce single-syllable words by blending sounds (phonemes), including consonant blends.
  - Isolate and pronounce initial, medial vowel, and final sounds (phonemes) in spoken single-syllable words.
  - Segment spoken single-syllable words into their complete sequence of individual sounds (phonemes).

Phonics and Word Recognition

- RF.1.3. Know and apply grade-level phonics and word-analysis skills in decoding words.
  - Know the spelling-sound correspondences for common consonant digraphs (two letters that represent one sound).

○ Decode regularly spelled one-syllable words.

○ Know final -e and common vowel team conventions for representing long vowel sounds.

○ Use knowledge that every syllable must have a vowel sound to determine the number of syllables in a printed word.

○ Decode two-syllable words following basic patterns by breaking the words into syllables.

○ Read words with inflectional endings.

○ Recognize and read grade-appropriate irregularly spelled words.

Fluency

- RF.1.4. Read with sufficient accuracy and fluency to support comprehension.

○ Read grade-level text with purpose and understanding.

○ Read grade-level text orally with accuracy, appropriate rate, and expression.

○ Use context to confirm or self-correct word recognition and understanding, rereading as necessary.

Writing

Text Types and Purposes

- W.1.1. Write opinion pieces in which they introduce the topic or name the book they are writing about, state an opinion, supply a reason for the opinion, and provide some sense of closure.

- W.1.2. Write informative/explanatory texts in which they name a topic, supply some facts about the topic, and provide some sense of closure.

- W.1.3. Write narratives in which they recount two or more appropriately sequenced events, include some details regarding what happened, use temporal words to signal event order, and provide some sense of closure.

Production and Distribution of Writing

- W.1.4. (Begins in Grade 3)
- W.1.5. With guidance and support from adults, focus on a topic, respond to questions and suggestions from peers, and add details to strengthen writing as needed.
- W.1.6. With guidance and support from adults, use a variety of digital tools to produce and publish writing, including in collaboration with peers.

Research to Build and Present Knowledge

- W.1.7. Participate in shared research and writing projects (e.g., explore a number of "how-to" books on a given topic and use them to write a sequence of instructions).
- W.1.8. With guidance and support from adults, recall information from experiences or gather information from provided sources to answer a question.
- W.1.9. (Begins in Grade 4)

Range of Writing

- W.1.10. (Begins in Grade 3)

Speaking and Listening

Comprehension and Collaboration

- SL.1.1. Participate in collaborative conversations with diverse partners about *Grade 1 topics and texts* with peers and adults in small and larger groups.
  - Follow agreed-upon rules for discussions (e.g., listening to others with care, speaking one at a time about the topics and texts under discussion).
  - Build on others' talk in conversations by responding to the comments of others through multiple exchanges.
  - Ask questions to clear up any confusion about the topics and texts under discussion.
- SL.1.2. Ask and answer questions about key details in a text read aloud or information presented orally or through other media.
- SL.1.3. Ask and answer questions about what a speaker says in order to gather additional information or clarify something that is not understood.

Presentation of Knowledge and Ideas

- SL.1.4. Describe people, places, things, and events with relevant details, expressing ideas and feelings clearly.
- SL.1.5. Add drawings or other visual displays to descriptions when appropriate to clarify ideas, thoughts, and feelings.
- SL.1.6. Produce complete sentences when appropriate to task and situation.

Language

Conventions of Standard English

- L.1.1. Demonstrate command of the conventions of standard English grammar and usage when writing or speaking.
  - Print all upper- and lowercase letters.
  - Use common, proper, and possessive nouns.
  - Use singular and plural nouns with matching verbs in basic sentences (e.g., He hops; We hop).
  - Use personal, possessive, and indefinite pronouns (e.g., I, me, my; they, them, their, anyone, everything).
  - Use verbs to convey a sense of past, present, and future (e.g., Yesterday I walked home; Today I walk home; Tomorrow I will walk home).
  - Use frequently occurring adjectives.
  - Use frequently occurring conjunctions (e.g., *and, but, or, so, because*).
  - Use determiners (e.g., articles, demonstratives).
  - Use frequently occurring prepositions (e.g., *during, beyond, toward*).
  - Produce and expand complete simple and compound declarative, interrogative, imperative, and exclamatory sentences in response to prompts.
- L.1.2. Demonstrate command of the conventions of standard English capitalization, punctuation, and spelling when writing.
  - Capitalize dates and names of people.
  - Use end punctuation for sentences.
  - Use commas in dates and to separate single words in a series.
  - Use conventional spelling for words with common spelling patterns and for frequently occurring irregular words.
  - Spell untaught words phonetically, drawing on phonemic awareness and spelling conventions.

Knowledge of Language

- L.1.3. (Begins in Grade 2)

Vocabulary Acquisition and Use

- L.1.4. Determine or clarify the meaning of unknown and multiple-meaning words and phrases based on *Grade 1 reading and content*, choosing flexibly from an array of strategies.
  - Use sentence-level context as a clue to the meaning of a word or phrase.
  - Use frequently occurring affixes as a clue to the meaning of a word.

○ Identify frequently occurring root words (e.g., *look*) and their inflectional forms (e.g., *looks, looked, looking*).

- L.1.5. With guidance and support from adults, demonstrate under-standing of figurative language, word relationships and nuances in word meanings.
  ○ Sort words into categories (e.g., colors, clothing) to gain a sense of the concepts the categories represent.
  ○ Define words by category and by one or more key attributes (e.g., a *duck* is a bird that swims; a *tiger* is a large cat with stripes).
  ○ Identify real-life connections between words and their use (e.g., note places at home that are *cozy*).
  ○ Distinguish shades of meaning among verbs differing in manner (e.g., *look, peek, glance, stare, glare, scowl*) and adjectives differing in intensity (e.g., large, gigantic) by defining or choosing them or by acting out the meanings.
- L.1.6. Use words and phrases acquired through conversations, reading and being read to, and responding to texts, including using frequently occurring conjunctions to signal simple relation-ships (e.g., *because*).

The study group had grown. Seeing the more experienced teachers collaborating and vigorously debating, Ms. Sanchez started sitting with them at lunch. She'd been a third-grade teacher for only 2 years but was excited by the rigor of their work. Feeling overwhelmed by her attempts to cover the entire third-grade curriculum, she was hopeful that maybe there was a better way.

They scrutinized the GLCEs, the power standards, and the CCSS. In short order they rejected the GLCEs as a source of powerful ongoing assessment or as a source of learning objectives for a thoughtful literacy curriculum. There were simply too many objectives, many of them were obtuse, and more seemed developmentally inappropriate for many of the children in a specific grade level. Trying to cover them all will dilute the effectiveness of instruction and deny the opportunity for quality learning and deep understanding of essential content and skills. The 5-inch binder with the entire set of first-grade GLCEs was put away in a dark closet, next to the 1978 magnetic strip card reader Mrs. Peterson had inherited from the teacher who once worked in her classroom.

The teachers now began to consider the relative values of the CCSS and the state's power standards. There were many similarities in the literacy sections. Both sets of outcomes were much fewer and more focused than the GLCEs. They were looking for answers to the questions that now served as their guide. What are the most important skills, content,

State Power Standards	Common Core State Standards
Provide much better focus for instruction than GLCEs	Provide much better focus for instruction than GLCEs
Vary significantly from state to state, and may not line up with international comparisons	Align with international comparisons
Available in all major subject areas	Only Literacy and Mathematics standards are available at this time
Occasionally vague or unclear language describing the learning objective	Clear, understandable language to describe the learning objective
Often unclear as to what proficiency or deep understanding of the skill would look like in the classroom	Often unclear as to what proficiency or deep understanding of the skill would look like in the classroom
Way too many standards for quality on-going progress monitoring or formative assessment	Way too many standards for quality ongoing progress monitoring or formative assessment
Could provide a manageable focus for instructional planning/ curriculum guide	Could provide a manageable focus for instructional planning/curriculum guide
Does not give a clear focus on the skills and behaviors which are crucial for each student to learn to a level of deep understanding and application	Does not give a clear focus on the skills and behaviors which are crucial for each student to learn to a level of deep understanding and application

and behaviors to teach? What are the most important factors to consistently measure so that instruction can be quickly adjusted if it is poorly matched to student readiness? What skills and behaviors must we ensure each student has learned to a level of deep understanding and application?

Progress. The GLCEs were off the table, discarded to the bowels of a dusty cupboard. The power standards and CCSS offered a much more manageable guide for curriculum planning. These are the things to teach. Of the two sources, they quickly leaned toward the CCSS. Almost all the states had committed to move in this direction.

They'd found a better guide to curriculum planning, but still there were challenges. The CCSS did not provide answers to some of their guiding questions. What are the most important factors to consistently measure so that instruction can be quickly adjusted if it is poorly matched to student readiness? What skills and behaviors must we ensure each student has learned to a level of deep understanding and application?

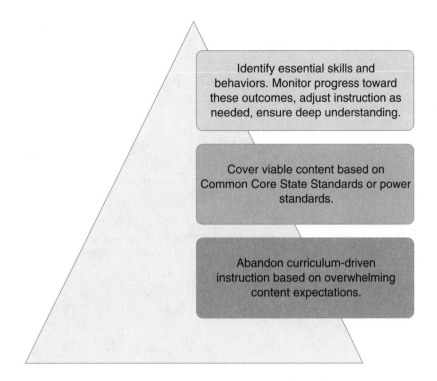

"Are we done yet?" asked Ms. Sanchez.

"I think we are done with the easy part," reflected Mrs. Samuels. "We've figured out how to narrow the focus of literacy instruction. We have a much better set of instructional goals to teach. But covering the material does not mean students have learned the material."

"We still need a manageable set of learning outcomes that we can vigilantly monitor and eventually ensure that each student will learn to that level of deep understanding and application. The CCSS moves us a long way in the right direction, but now we need to narrow the scope of our thinking from coverage to what children need to learn really well," added Mrs. Peterson.

"So we can go through the CCSS and pick the standards that are the crucial indicators?" offered Ms. Sanchez.

"With the CCSS and a little common sense, we can find the crucial literacy outcomes for which we'll measure student learning instead of coverage. These are the skills for which some kids need extra time or attention. These are the skills which we want to guarantee students have deeply learned and can easily use for years to come," answered Mrs. Peterson.

Ms. Sanchez frowned. "I'm feeling a little overwhelmed here," she admitted. "You're saying we should focus instruction on a viable curriculum, and we can find that with the guidance of the power standards or the common core standards."

"Right," answered Mrs. Samuels.

"That seems like a lot of work. All the materials and lesson plans I already have are based on covering all the GLCEs!" said the young third-grade teacher. "But you are also saying we need to identify an even more focused set of literacy learning outcomes and keep track of how students are progressing toward those outcomes?"

Mrs. Samuels could understand how she felt. "You're right. It will be a lot of work. But you'll have a chance to teach the more important skills and content to a deeper level of understanding, and then keep track of the crucial indicators as your students make progress."

"You will really help me? I'm going to need to narrow the focus of my curriculum, identify crucial literacy indicators, keep track of how students progress, and then adjust instruction to give kids more time on crucial skills or move them forward to new skills when they are ready!"

"We will," promised Mrs. Samuels and Mrs. Peterson. The veteran teachers glanced at each other.

"There's more, isn't there?" inquired Ms. Sanchez. "I can feel it."

"One step at a time," answered Mrs. Peterson. "We'll start with literacy."

"We'll focus on a viable literacy curriculum, identify crucial learning outcomes, and then figure out how to monitor progress and adjust instruction to give students enough time and help to achieve all the essential literacy outcomes," Mrs. Samuels promised. "It's a good start."

CHAPTER 3 STUDY QUESTIONS

1. What are the characteristics of a power standard?

2. Has your staff had deep conversations about the importance of power standards?

3. Analyze the CCSS for Grade 1 literacy. Are they a more concise set of learning outcomes than what is presently in use in your school? Is it clear what proficiency for each outcome might look like? Would a curriculum based on these standards be viable?

4. What are the differences between the state power standards and the CCSS?

5. From among the CCSS for literacy, how would you go about determining the crucial indicators of long-term literacy success?

6. How could you use Deming's ideas to improve teaching and learning in your school?

7. In what ways is teaching a more focused curriculum to a deeper level of understanding more challenging than typical curriculum-driven instruction?

Essential Skills and the Whole Child   4

"I thought we were going to focus just on literacy skills," said Mrs. Samuels to her friend after school.

"I'm struggling with that," replied Mrs. Peterson.

"You can't do everything all at once."

"Of course you are right, but I just can't seem to separate literacy from oral language, or visual motor skills, or phonologic skills. And for kids like Justin and Ralph, it sometimes seems that the biggest barrier to literacy is their behavior and social skills," she commiserated.

"You're making this complicated."

"I know. These kids are complicated. And their learning needs are complicated. And I am so frustrated that I don't have a system to put all the important pieces together," said Mrs. Peterson with a deep sigh.

For days she'd been struggling with it. The literacy part was easy. Mrs. Peterson had gone through the Common Core State Standards (CCSS) and found the skills that had the leverage to improve reading and writing outcomes. These were skills that once learned would endure over time and were clearly essential for success at the next grade level. When her list was still too long to carefully monitor progress, she rewrote and narrowed the objectives. The essential literacy skills began to stand out.

Essential Grade 1 Literacy Skills, First Draft

- Identifies uppercase letters
- Identifies lowercase letters
- Identifies a letter sound associated with each letter
- Recognizes basic grade-level sight words
- Follows print when reading (visual tracking)

- Decodes grade-appropriate print
- Reads short sentences with fluency
- Reads for meaning (not just word calling)
- Prints 30 to 50 personally meaningful words
- Expresses ideas in writing (simple sentences)
- Spells using common word patterns
- Spells words using visual memory

With a solid ability to use these skills, Mrs. Peterson could predict that students would be able to succeed in Grade 2. Most of her students could achieve even more than this set of skills, she was sure. But these were crucial.

It was when Mrs. Peterson had taken the list to school and began to consider which students were on track toward developing these skills that things got complicated. Danny, Justin, and Tyrel could barely hold a pencil. They got tired and fussy after just a few minutes of seat work. Junie, Peter, Cassandra, and Tyrel did not yet have the oral language vocabulary to understand the meaning of some of the grade-level sight words. Jessica was a puzzle. Her oral language was good, but her attention wandered; she slumped in her chair, rubbed her eyes all the time, and knocked into things as she moved around the classroom. Sarah and Phillip already had most of these essential outcomes in place, she realized. But Suzie, Samantha, Ralph, Joel, and Jason did not even know all their letters and sounds. And they wouldn't recognize a rhyme if it bit them on the leg.

She recognized that literacy could not be considered in isolation. "I wish it were that simple," she muttered to herself. Children with oral language delays, visual motor delays, gaps in the development of phonologic skills, or attention and behavior issues would struggle to develop the crucial literacy skills if she failed to address their other needs.

"Matthew," called Mrs. Peterson when she got home that day, "I need your help."

Her teenaged son answered from upstairs. "I am kind of busy."

"Come down anyway, my brilliant boy," she replied.

He bumped down the stairs.

With his mother's direction, Matthew searched for articles and information on essential grade-level phonologic skills, gross motor skills, visual motor skills, oral language, behavior skills, social skills, numeracy skills, and even a set of skills associated with preliteracy. After a couple of hours, they had found many references and printed dozens of articles. The information was piled high. Still Mrs. Peterson wanted more.

"I'm starving. Do you think we could have some dinner soon?" asked Matthew.

"I lost track of the time," his mother said.

Together, they began to prepare dinner. When Mr. Peterson arrived home, he cleaned up and joined them in the kitchen.

"What have you two been up to?" he inquired as he began to set the table.

"My head is full of school stuff. We should have a no school-talk dinner conversation tonight," she stated firmly. "I need to clear some space in my head."

Matthew and his father smiled quietly.

At the dinner table, Mrs. Peterson made a point to thank Matthew for his help.

"You really do know how to do basic searches on your own," he reminded his mom. "And next year I'll be away at college and harder to find when you need some free help."

"Maybe that can be one of our goals for this year." She smiled. "You can help me learn to be more technology independent."

"God help me," muttered Matthew. "Now it's the teenager's job to help his parents become independent before he leaves home!"

After dinner Mrs. Peterson began to sort through her references and articles, Mr. Peterson took the dog for a walk, and Matthew went upstairs to his studies.

For Mrs. Peterson, it seemed like beginning to work on a 5,000-piece jigsaw puzzle. There was so much information. Sorting the articles and book references into groups gave her some sense of progress. She was trying to organize information in a way that would help answer the question: What is essential for my first-grade students to learn? She considered the most valuable references she had collected over the years and blended them with newer journal articles and books that addressed the basic needs of children. But it was too much information (see Appendix B). She shifted strategies and pulled out only the articles and books that she saw as indispensable to a deep understanding of the needs of children in the early years of school. From these she hoped to cull the critical factors that would help her define success for her students.

Her list of indispensable sources was still daunting. It included articles or books on the development of literacy skills by Allington (2001); Clay (1985); Torgesen (1988); Vellutino, Scanlon, and Tanzman (1998); Marzano, Pickering, and Pollock (2001); Boyer (1995); Snow (1998); and Jensen (2005). Next to this stack she placed articles and references for instructional match and included Gickling and Armstrong (1978), Tucker (2001), Kovaleski (1995), Fuchs (1992), and Vygotsky (1978).

Sources describing essential phonologic skills included Kaminski (2007), Speece (2004), and Snow (2005). Oral language skill references included Healy (1999), Chomsky (1976), Hart (2003), Risley (1995), Shaywitz (2004), and Stanovich (1994).

The reference stack for essential early gross motor skills included Hannaford (2005), Dennison (1986), Liddle (2003), Ratey (2008), and Jensen (2005). Next to that emerged the visual motor skills references, including Ayres (2005), Hannaford (2005), Sornson (2010), Rayner (1997), Kranowitz (2005), and Rourke (1995).

Numeracy references included Thomas, Tagg, and Ward (2002); Bobis (2008); and Anghileri (2006).

It was difficult for her to choose from among the many important behavior and social skills references. So much important work described the critical development of these skills, but she was determined to find a manageable frame of reference from which to determine essential outcomes. Mrs. Peterson sorted until her reference materials included Fay, Cline, and Sornson (2000); Cline and Fay (1990); Horner, Sugai, and Homer (2000); Glasser (1969); Adler (1956); Bondy and Ross (2008); Goleman (1995); and Coloroso (1995).

One last pile of information kept growing. At first it was a miscellaneous stack of interesting articles and book references. Eventually, it became Mrs. Peterson's file on the importance of taking into account the whole child when considering learning priorities. In this file, she kept materials describing the work of Brazelton and Greenspan (2000); Weikart, Bond, and McNeil (1978); Sylwester (1995); Jensen (2005); Caine (1991); Healy (1999); Boyer (1995); Elias (1976); Kline (1988); Gregorc (1984); Comer (1989); Kagan (1990, 2001); Vygotsky (1978); Montessori (1967); Piaget (1952); and Erikson (1959).

With the articles and books organized in front of her, chosen from the still greater set of resources she dearly valued, Mrs. Peterson felt weary and overwhelmed. She was committed to helping each child develop as a whole child in her classroom, knowing that every piece of the puzzle was indispensable to long-term learning success. But the lists of important learning outcomes were already too long, and it was easy to keep adding and adding content and skills to her expectations for her students.

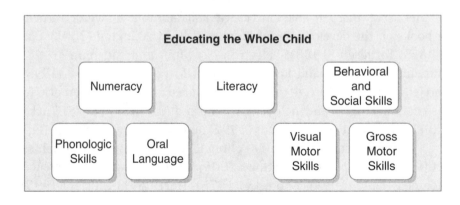

It was almost midnight on Saturday and she was too tired to continue. As she finished her work for the night and moved wearily upstairs to bed, she saw Matthew in the family room still working on his laptop.

"It's late. You should be in bed," she groused at him.

"Almost done," he said.

"No, really. It's late," she said in her teacher voice.

"I'm not tired. I just have a little more to do."

She was dog-tired and a little cranky. Part of her wanted to snarl at him and send him to bed. Another part recognized that her 6-foot 3-inch boy was going off to college next year. Bedtime would be unsupervised. "What are you working on?" she inquired.

"Just a little project."

"For one of your classes?" she asked.

"No, just something I've been working on."

"Do you care to share?" she asked her son.

"Sure. How about tomorrow? I'm almost ready to share," he answered.

It was after dinner the next evening before he completed his project and called her into the family room. He had a file folder with printouts next to his computer.

"You've been busting your butt working on your first-grade progress monitoring system," he began.

She eyed her son suspiciously. "Yes, I have. I'm sorry it's been taking so much time. Is there a problem?"

"Yes, I suppose there is. You've been trying to pull together all the pieces, and that is a lot of work."

"No kidding," she replied. "At the present rate it'll take me all year."

"And then you'll have to try it out and work out all the kinks. This thing could take forever," he said thoughtfully.

"Are you trying to discourage me? I am already feeling overwhelmed," she admitted.

Her son just smiled. "No. I figured someone must have done this before. But I couldn't find the right keywords to lead me to it. So I asked Alex to help me, and we've been scouring the electronic world to find something simple enough to use that monitors the progress of all the essential skills you've been researching."

Mrs. Peterson heard her husband enter the family room and sit down on the chair behind her, but she stayed focused on her son. "Really?"

"Yeah. We found something good a few days ago," he began, but his mother interrupted him.

"And you didn't show me?"

"It took a few days to get everything we needed, and that's where Dad comes in," answered her son.

She glanced at her husband, but he just put on his inscrutable look. She looked back to her son.

"We found something called *The Essential Skills Inventories* that monitors progress toward language, literacy, numeracy, phonologic skills, gross motor, visual motor, and social and behavior skills [Sornson, 2012]." Matthew explained. He handed her a copy of the list of skills monitored for first grade. "It's the only working system we could find. You may decide to create your own set of essential outcomes, but I figured this would cut way down on your work."

FIRST-GRADE ESSENTIAL SKILLS INVENTORY

Letters

- Identifies uppercase letters
- Identifies lowercase letters

Phonologic Skills

- Identifies a letter sound associated with each letter
- Produces rhymes for a given word
- Identifies beginning, middle, and ending sounds of words
- Combines phonemes to make words

Language

- Uses age-appropriate vocabulary in speech
- Uses language to solve problems
- Demonstrates effective listening skills

Motor Skills

- Demonstrates appropriate balance
- Demonstrates appropriate skipping
- Uses comfortable near-point vision

Visualization

- Draws pictures with detail
- Can tell/retell a story

Literacy

- Recognizes basic sight words
- Follows print when reading (visual tracking)
- Decodes grade-appropriate print

- Reads short sentences
- Reads for meaning
- Prints 30 to 50 personally meaningful words
- Expresses ideas in writing (simple sentences)
- Spells using common word patterns
- Spells words using visual memory

Numeracy

- Counts objects with accuracy to 100
- Replicates visual patterns or movement patterns
- Recognizes number groups without counting (2–10)
- Understands concepts of add on or take away (to 30) with manipulatives
- Can add or subtract single digit problems on paper
- Shows a group of objects by number (to 100)

Behavior

- Delays gratification when necessary
- Plays well with others
- Shows interest in learning

"Here is a copy of a classroom inventory with some data already inserted as a model"—he handed her another printout—"and here is a rubric that describes the levels of skill that lead to proficiency. And here is a protocol for how to use it. And here is an individual folder you can use for a specific student."

Her son paused to let her briefly digest all this.

"I thought you'd want to keep an electronic file and that wasn't available. So here is a license that Dad got from the author that allows you to use the spreadsheet I put together for you." Matthew turned the computer toward her to show her the database system that he'd built to let her update the information electronically. It had her name on the top and all her students listed.

"We know how much you want to do this right," offered Matthew with a grin. "And we hope this helps."

> Out of intense complexities simplicities emerge.
>
> Winston Churchill

The study group continued to meet twice a week after school, and most days at lunch. Mrs. Samuels and Ms. Sanchez were concentrated on narrowing the second- and third-grade literacy focus to a viable curriculum. Another second-grade teacher, Mrs. Jackson, became interested and decided to join them.

In her first-grade classroom, Mrs. Peterson began collecting baseline data for all her students. She observed them carefully, and devised instructional activities that gave her specific information to help her see which of her students already had developed proficiency in each of the essential skills. A pattern began to emerge. She could clearly see the groups of children who needed more time developing any of the skills. She could see which students were already solid in a skill area and ready to move on to more challenging work. She could see which skills were appropriate for whole-class instruction, because almost all the students still had a long way to go before achieving proficiency.

In the lunchroom, a few of the other teachers made comments about all the energy they were giving to this project. "Is this a district curriculum committee or something?" someone asked. Mrs. Samuels explained that it was not. They were just exploring narrowing the curricular focus to a set of viable teaching outcomes. "Is it a PLC?" another teacher asked. Mrs. Samuels explained that it was not an official committee of any kind. "Is there a stipend for meeting after school?" No, there is not.

At their next after-school meeting there was a knock on the door, and then Mrs. Rhodes walked in. She was a tall and strongly built woman, had been a kindergarten teacher in the district for more than 30 years, and had an undeserved reputation for being brusque. It was said that she had been asked many years ago to become a principal but had refused. She seldom spoke at staff meetings, but when she did, her thoughts were clear and concise. She refused to join district committees and had once described committee work as a way to accelerate brain cell death. In her kindergarten classroom, she was content. It was a classroom in which children flourished. Mrs. Rhodes seldom came to the lunchroom. She didn't have time, she explained, and usually ate in her class.

"Is this the noncommittee I've heard about?" she asked upon entering Mrs. Peterson's room.

"Yes, I suppose it is," said Mrs. Peterson with a laugh.

"Could you tell me what you are working on?" asked Mrs. Rhodes.

Mrs. Samuels and Ms. Sanchez explained their efforts to focus on a viable literacy curriculum, identify crucial learning outcomes, and then figure out how to monitor progress and adjust instruction to give students enough time and help to achieve all the essential literacy outcomes.

"That sounds right. I've never taken those GLCEs seriously anyway," explained Mrs. Rhodes. Somehow they could imagine it was true.

Mrs. Rhodes was sitting in a tiny first-grade chair, and her large frame looked incongruous balanced on the tiny seat. She was sitting next to Mrs. Peterson, whose classroom inventory was in front of her on the table. "What's all this?" she asked, pointing at the inventory with its data showing which children had demonstrated proficiency on the first-grade essential skills.

Explaining the inventory, Mrs. Peterson showed her which students had already demonstrated proficiency in each of the first-grade skills.

"And if a student has not yet demonstrated proficiency, you still have a blank spot on the inventory for that skill?" she asked. "And that skill continues to be a focus for instruction?"

"Exactly. The goal is to help each child be proficient in each essential skill by the end of the year," said Mrs. Peterson.

"And when they are proficient, what then?"

"Then it's time to move on to more advanced learning goals," explained the first-grade teacher.

Mrs. Rhodes continued studying Mrs. Peterson's first-grade inventory. She pointed to the numeracy section. "All these kids who have proficient number sense, we sure worked hard on that last year," said Mrs. Rhodes. She found Jimmy's name, and followed the row to the blank frame under "*recognizes number groups without counting (2–10).*"

"We worked hard on this skill last year, but Jimmy never quite mastered it," said Mrs. Rhodes softly. She looked at Mrs. Peterson. "Second and third grade are focusing on literacy, but you are looking at every aspect of development on this inventory."

"She's an overachiever," interjected Mrs. Samuels. "She's been stressing herself."

"I wanted to look at the whole child," Mrs. Peterson responded. "And fortunately I've had a lot of help both here and at home."

The kindergarten teacher adjusted her large frame on the tiny first-grade chair. "Now this is something I could get excited about. May I join your noncommittee?" asked Mrs. Rhodes.

CHAPTER 4 STUDY QUESTIONS

1. Consider the *Essential Grade 1 Literacy Skills* that Mrs. Peterson developed after her review of the Common Core State Standards. Do these skills represent a solid base of literacy skills that meet Ainsworth's criteria for power standards?

2. Why was it difficult for Mrs. Peterson to focus on literacy skills without also considering the development of oral language, phonologic skills, motor skills, and social skills?

3. What is the connection between oral language and literacy skills?

4. What do you mean by *educating the whole child?*

5. There are 32 items on the First-Grade Essential Skills Inventory. Are there any learning objectives on this list that you do not understand or consider nonessential?

THE K–3 ESSENTIAL SKILLS INVENTORIES

Any state education agency or county or large district education agency with sufficient resources to develop and maintain a database for the Essential Skills Inventory is invited to obtain a free license to use these materials in electronic form. The license will include a commitment to the staff training necessary for successful implementation of these materials for formative assessment and responsive instruction. For information, contact the author at **earlylearningfoundation.com.**

The Challenge of Formative Assessment and Responsive Instruction 5

"Is everyone ready to learn today?" asked Mrs. Peterson as part of her morning routine. Every child smiled at her and answered clearly, "Yes I am!"

And the learning began. During morning meeting, Mrs. Peterson asked Peter to tell the class what he did over the weekend. But he was so shy, and words came so hard for him. "Tell us about the zoo," she prodded, remembering that his family was planning a visit on Saturday. But he looked away and shifted his feet nervously, and she gently excused him and moved on to another more verbal student.

For math that day, Mrs. Peterson had devised a terrific lesson that included recognizing a number value that she presented as a pattern of dots on a large flashcard, then tapped the value of the number on the top of the worktables. But Jimmy, Tyrel, Junie, and Samantha could not begin to keep up, while Sarah and Phillip just looked bored. The teacher quickly transitioned to an addition activity that allowed the students to work in groups to solve a problem on the abacus and then write the solution on a worksheet. This activity went much better at first, but soon there was bedlam in the corner where Tyrel's group was working. Moving quickly to the group, she found Danny, Samantha, and Justin vocalizing their anger at Tyrel, who had scribbled numbers all over the group's worksheet.

"He's just scribbling all over our worksheet," complained Samantha. "He's going to get all of us in trouble."

Trying not to meet the teacher's gaze, Tyrel at first refused to explain. But then Mrs. Peterson realized the problem. The math problems on the worksheets were printed in small size. Mrs. Peterson had assigned Tyrel the job of recording the group's answers. And he had managed to print the answers sloppily but accurately for the first row of problems, but Tyrel's printing skills were poor, and his hand and eyes had grown weary from the task of printing such tiny numbers. His eyes were now filled with tears, and she could not know if that was from the visual strain of the job she'd given him or the embarrassment of letting his frustration show in front of the group. Joining the group, Mrs. Peterson allowed the students to start over using a clean worksheet, and she wrote the answers as they discovered them on the abacus. After the group was working happily again, she assigned Jimmy the job of recording answers and began circulating again through the classroom.

At the end of recess that morning, Mrs. Peterson decided to tell all her students to wait for the whistle and then skip across the playground to get in line by the classroom door. At the whistle they stopped still, waited for the teacher's signal, and began to skip from wherever they were playing across the grounds. Sarah led the way with her beautiful, fluid skipping motion. Many others skipped well, followed by a collection of the weirdest gallops and hops imaginable. The teacher laughed inwardly at the picture, until somehow coming across the soft dirt near the swing set, Junie and Tyrel both lost their balance within their awkward gallops and stumbled hard into the dirt. Mrs. Peterson and several of the students ran quickly to help them.

After lunch, things finally found a productive rhythm within the first-grade classroom. It was quiet reading time, and Mrs. Peterson was helping Jessica when Jason began tugging on her pant leg, insisting on her attention.

"I need to talk to you," Jason insisted.

For Jason it was always hard to wait. "Do you need to go to the bathroom?" checked Mrs. Peterson.

He shook his head. "No. I just need to get another book."

"You can go back to your seat. I'll come talk to you in a moment."

"Now," said Jason as he stomped one foot.

"At first grade we practice waiting our turn, Jason. Go to your seat, please. I'll come talk to you in a moment."

Starting to pout, Jason turned away, then turned back to face his teacher. "You have to talk to me now. My mother said you have to talk to me whenever I want," he yelled.

As Mrs. Peterson led Jason out into the hallway to discuss this behavior, she realized he had just found a way to get the attention he wanted. But in that moment there weren't many options. She wondered how she would find a way to help him control his emotions and behaviors, learn to delay gratification, and figure out which behaviors would help him succeed in school and in life. Punishment was always an option to consider when facing poor behaviors, she realized, but most of the time first-grade behavioral problems reflected a lack of emotional control, social skills, and knowing what good school behavior really looks like. There were many learning steps between where Jason was on that day, and where he needed to someday be to help him have the behavior skills to be a successful person.

So many differences. So many needs.

With two-and-a-half decades of experience teaching young students, Mrs. Peterson knew that teaching a rigid one-size-fits-all curriculum was so much easier than trying to teach responsively to the needs of her individual students. Lessons designed to cover content are done the moment the lesson is over, while responsive instruction requires progress monitoring to see which children actually learned the skills or content, followed by re-teaching to students who failed to fully learn your lesson, followed by more monitoring to see if the skill has yet been learned, followed by more intensive support and practice until crucial skills are proficient.

She also knew that angry or intimidating behavior management could scare kids like Jason into some form of compliance. But compliance is far different than helping students learn to willingly follow classroom procedures, choose behaviors that make the class safe for everyone, and learn appropriate social skills for play and for dealing with adult authority figures.

In most schools, a teacher can choose to intimidate kids into good behavior and cover content whether it is well learned or not learned at all. But Mrs. Peterson had made a promise. She had posted her promise on the bulletin board next to her desk. Now she was trying to learn to assess students to determine what they knew so she could plan to teach them what they need to learn at the correct level of difficulty.

IN MY CLASSROOM

All my students will develop the skills and behaviors they need to succeed.

Each child will get the time needed to develop the essential skills.

I will offer essential instruction at the correct instructional level.

In my class, children will feel physically and emotionally safe.

I will help children discover the importance and joy of learning.

Each day, children will experience positive relationships, respect, empathy, and love.

Assessment options can be roughly divided into two categories: formative assessments and summative assessments. *Formative assessments* are on-going assessments, reviews, and observations in a classroom that teachers use to help them understand the needs of students and to plan instruction. Formative assessments include teacher observation, anecdotal records, running records, examination of work samples, progress monitoring of essential skills, diagnostic tests, and quizzes or assignments that help the teacher judge student skill levels to help her plan instruction (Popham, 2003). Formative assessment delivers information *during* the instructional process, allowing both the teacher and the student use the information to plan or improve further learning (Reeves, 2004). It is an ongoing and dynamic process. It could include an assessment of what has been already learned, where there are gaps, how the student learns best, and what motivates this student to learn. The use of formative assessment improves learning (Black & Wiliam, 1998).

The key to the value of formative assessment is the actions of the teacher based on this information. The primary function of formative assessments is not to grade students, but rather to inform the teacher about what the student knows and can do, thereby allowing the teacher to design instruction that is well matched to student needs and readiness.

Summative assessments are used to evaluate learning at the end of a teaching unit, or a marking period, or some other unit of time. The goal of summative assessments is to make a judgment about the student's learning after an instructional phase is complete. Summative assessments support giving a yearly grade, or assigning a percentile score on an achievement test, support a score given on a diagnostic assessment, or give a score on an entrance test like the SAT or ACT.

> Summative assessments give students a score. Formative assessments give teachers and students information to help them plan instruction.

Think of formative assessment as *assessment for learning* (Stiggins, Arter, Chappuis, & Chappuis, 2006). When there are clear learning goals that are considered important by both the teacher and the learner, formative assessment can help the student answer these important questions (Atkin, Black, & Coffey, 2001):

- What am I attempting to learn? What does a good product or performance look like?
- Where am I now? How does this compare with the desired outcome?
- How can I close the gap? Am I making progress?

Stiggins (2002) describes the differences between formative assessment and assessment for learning. Formative assessment is an important part of assessment for learning; however, "assessment for learning is far more than testing more frequently or providing teachers with evidence so they can revise instruction" (p. 5). Feedback is one of the critical components of assessment for learning and, given as part of assessment for learning, helps learners know where their understandings or skills have "broken down" and provides actions necessary to get them back "on track" with the desired learning goal. The most helpful kind of feedback provides specific comments about errors and specific suggestions for improvement. Stiggins (2002) calls this descriptive feedback versus judgmental feedback.

Leahy and colleagues (2005) define other critical features of assessment for learning in addition to providing feedback that moves learners forward. These include involving students in assessing their own learning, making sure students understand before teaching what the learning goals are and what "success" looks like, using peer assessing, and initiating discussions.

Having decided to help all her students achieve essential learning outcomes, Mrs. Peterson was now learning to manage data that would allow her to keep track of which students achieved essential skills and which ones still needed more time and practice to develop these skills. She was learning to manage formative data to guide her instruction toward the remarkable goal of helping all her students achieve the foundation skills needed for successful on-going learning, rather than using summative data with the primary purpose of giving children grades. She was learning to use *formative assessment* to help her plan *responsive instruction.*

Responsive instruction assumes that educators have developed a viable curriculum and identified crucial learning outcomes. By focusing on the essential skills and behaviors, and carefully monitoring progress toward those standards, we encourage teachers to help children develop a deep understanding of essential concepts and skills. Teachers are able to easily identify which essential skills students have already learned or still need to learn. Teachers are able to offer instruction, reteaching, and additional practice time as needed, in response to the specific needs of students, at a level of difficulty that allows for a good instructional match.

Rather than using formative assessment and responsive instruction sporadically within her classroom, Mrs. Peterson was learning to use them systematically and carefully to ensure that her students truly learned the essential outcomes.

Although she did her best to "cover" all the Common Core State Standards, she was vigilant to collect data regarding which students demonstrated proficiency for the Essential Skills. For more than a month, she gathered her baseline data while transforming her curriculum plan to focus on CCSS outcomes.

Most of the data collection relied on teacher observation. While on the playground, she could observe which children could skip and which could play well with others. She already knew which children knew all their letters and letter sounds. On her inventory she carefully recorded which students could produce rhymes and use the other phonologic skills with proficiency. Oral language skills took more thought to allow her to carefully assess her students' baseline skills. Some students were more naturally reticent, and had better spoken language skills than she might have guessed. She observed and took notes during morning meetings and during class discussions. Occasionally, she pulled a small group together for discussion. She compared her notes and observations with the rubric for proficiency. Her skills as a teacher of literacy skills served her well as she used running records and other observational assessments to help her gather baseline data for reading and writing skills. Mrs. Rhodes helped her develop some simple activities to determine which students could tell or retell stories from reading and from personal experience. Mrs. Samuels helped her develop some simple lessons that gave her good information on math skills. Behavioral skills were measured through teacher observation, being mindful of the standards in the Essential Skills Rubric.

Once baseline data were gathered, she began in earnest to plan her teaching plan on Common Core objectives in combination with the needs presented by her class of students. Whole-group instruction was devised so that everyone could benefit. Practice time and reteaching time were planned with specific learning needs in mind. She found herself mindful of which students could be matched for small group instruction for math. Reading groups were formed with students with similar skills, and oral language activity groups were formed with students of mixed ability. Mrs. Peterson had shifted from offering lessons based on covering hundreds of GLCEs to instruction based on a more focused curriculum and the specific learning needs of her students.

As she expected, the range of skills in her class was astounding. Even before the end of the first marking period, both Sarah and Phillip had demonstrated proficiency in every first-grade essential literacy, language, phonologic, and motor skill. Mrs. Peterson scrambled to find materials and activities that could offer them the appropriate level of challenge.

The pattern of interconnected skills especially interested the first-grade teacher. Most of the children with oral language delays were also struggling in literacy, but also with social skills. Most of the children with gross motor skill delays were also delayed in the development of visual motor skills, and most of the children with visual motor delays weren't very good at drawing with detail or retelling stories. Some of the students with advanced academic skills had difficulty following classroom rules and playing well with others. Mrs. Peterson was developing a clearer picture of her students than she had ever had in the past.

For most of her students, the experienced first-grade teacher could imagine a path to full proficiency in each of the essential skills, but for some the path was less clear. Junie and Tyrel had the greatest language delays, and this impacted their readiness in phonologic skills, literacy skills, social skills, and even numeracy. Justin, Junie, Danny, and Tyrel still struggled with balance and skipping, and could barely catch a small beanbag. They were making progress, but it was slow in comparison with the rest of the class. A few of the students had quirky patterns of gaps. Justin had good language skills but struggled with listening and problem solving. Joel had gaps in rhyming, balancing, drawing with detail, and math. Andrew was a positive leader in the class, but had an aversion to math and seemed to tune out during math instruction. Jessica was perhaps her greatest cipher, with lovely oral language skills that she only used one-to-one, and a tendency to withdraw gently to another place. She was always so sweet when Mrs. Peterson guided her to get reengaged in the classroom learning activity.

Some observers might say that Mrs. Peterson was using more differentiated instruction in this year's first-grade classroom, but Mrs. Peterson would offer a different view. She'd always differentiated instruction in her class, based on learning styles, interests, and levels of skill. But now her instruction was differentiated with specific knowledge of the pattern of skills her students had already developed and focused on giving them instruction at the correct level of difficulty to maximize learning for each of the essential skills.

Jimmy and Tyrel were working with Mrs. Peterson on basic number combinations using an abacus. After a moment, Tyrel looked up at his teacher with a sad expression.

"My dad said he was never good at math either," Tyrel said with a tone of resignation.

"My dad said math is really important, and I'd better learn it or I'll never get a job," interjected Jimmy.

Mrs. Peterson tried to get the lesson back on track. "OK, Jimmy. Let's try another problem. Show me 18."

"Maybe we're just not very good at this stuff," said Tyrel.

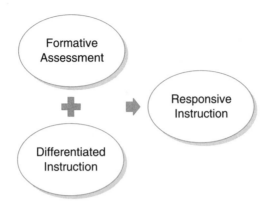

"Nice try, Tyrel. You are on track to being an excellent math student. It's not even the end of the first marking period, and you are halfway to learning all the essential math skills," explained Mrs. Peterson.

"No way."

"Oh, yes."

"Mrs. Peterson, what will we be able to do by the end of the year?" asked Jimmy.

The teacher looked around, and called Ralph over to the table. Indicating the abacus, Mrs. Peterson said, "Ralph, show me 18."

He quickly complied.

"Now add 12 more," she said to Ralph.

He quickly added 12 more.

"How many do you have now?" she asked.

Ralph answered correctly. They did a few more combination problems using numbers up to 30. Then, again using the abacus, Mrs. Peterson had Ralph show several number values up to 100 on the counting frame. She excused Ralph and sent him back to his work.

"What do you think?" she asked the boys. "Do you think you'll be able to do that kind of problem before long?"

"Heck, yeah," they both said together. "Is that all we have to learn?"

Shaking her head, she laughed. "No, there is a little bit more than that. But the problems Ralph just answered are the hardest part of what you absolutely have to learn this year in math. And it will take some practice to get supergood at math, so let's get at it."

CHAPTER 5 STUDY QUESTIONS

1. What is the difference between formative and summative assessment? Give an example of each.

2. How can students use formative assessment?

3. In your own words, what is responsive instruction?

4. What is the connection between differentiated instruction and responsive instruction?

5. List all the different summative assessments used in your school. Can any of them be used to effectively help teachers plan instruction?

Teacher: Mrs. Peterson Baseline Data

Indicate mastery by writing mastery date to the right of the student's name and under the feature mastered

Area of Assessment / Essential Skills	Letters		Phonologic Skills				Language			Motor Skills			Visualization			
	1	2	3	4	5	6	7	8	9	10	11	12	13	14	15	16
Student Name /	Identifies uppercase letters	Identifies lowercase letters	Identifies a letter sound associated with each letter	Produces rhymes for a given word	Identifies beginning, middle, and ending sounds of words	Combines phonemes to make words	Uses age-appropriate vocabulary in speech	Uses language to solve problems	Demonstrates effective listening skills	Demonstrates appropriate balance	Demonstrates appropriate skipping	Uses comfortable near-point vision	Draws pictures with detail	Can tell or retell a story	Recognizes basic sight words	Follows print when reading (visual tracking)
Phillip	9–28	9–28	10–3	10–20	10–26	10–26	10–1	10–25		10–1	10–1	10–1		10–15		10–18
Jimmy	9–28	10–8	10–15	10–15				10–14	10–14					10–20		
Sarah	9–28	9–28	10–3	10–20	10–26	10–26	10–1	10–2	10–2	10–1	10–1	10–1	10–18	10–15		10–18
Abigail	10–15	10–30		10–15				10–14	10–14							
Kendra	10–15	10–15	10–15						10–18		10–1	10–1		10–18		10–18
Danny	9–28	9–28			10–26				10–14					10–18		
Junie	10–30															
Justin	9–28	9–28														
Tyrel	10–30	10–30														
Peter	9–28	9–28								10–18						10–18
Cassandra	9–28	9–28							10–14	10–18			10–18			10–18
Jessica	10–7	10–23	10–23											10–20		10–18
Suzie	9–28	9–28	10–15		10–26					10–1		10–1	10–16			10–18
Ralph	9–28	9–28	10–15		10–26					10–1		10–1				10–18
Joel	9–28	9–28	10–15								10–1					
Jason	9–28	9–28	10–15													
Justin	9–28	9–28	10–15	10–15	10–26					10–1	10–1		10–16			10–18
Samantha	9–28	9–28	10–3	10–15	10–26					10–1	10–1		10–16			10–18
Andrew	9–28	9–28	10–15													
Marcus	9–28	9–28	10–15													
Dylan	9–28	9–28	10–15							10–1						
Camilla	9–28	9–28	10–3	10–15	10–26				10–14	10–1	10–1	10–1	10–16			10–18
Katie	9–28	9–28	10–3	10–15	10–26				10–14	10–1	10–1	10–1	10–16			10–18

	Literacy							Numeracy						Behavior		
17	18	19	20	21	22	23	24	25	26	27	28	29	30	31	32
Decodes grade-appropriate print	Reads short sentences	Reads for meaning	Prints 30 to 50 personally meaningful words	Expresses ideas in writing (simple sentences)	Spells using common word patterns	Spells words using visual memory	Counts objects with accuracy to 100	Replicates visual patterns or movement patterns	Recognizes number groups without counting (2 to 10)	Understands concepts of add on or take away (to 30) with manipulatives	Adds/subtracts single digit problems on paper	Shows a group of objects by number (to 100)	Delays gratification when necessary	Plays well with others	Shows interest in learning
10–4	10–18		10–4	10–4	10–18		10–22	10–19	9–25		10–6		10–15		10–1
									10–14				10–8	10–5	10–1
10–4	10–18		10–4	10–4	10–18		10–25	10–19	9–14		10–6		10–1	10–5	10–1
									10–14				10–8	10–5	10–5
							10–26						10–15		
							10–26						10–15		
							10–26								
10–25							10–25	10–19	9–14				10–15		
10–25							10–22	10–19	9–25				10–15	10–15	
10–18			10–8	10–8	10–18		10–22	10–19	9–25						
							10–22	10–19	10–14						
							10–22		9–25						10–5
							10–22		9–25						
10–4	10–18		10–8	10–8	10–18		10–22	10–19	9–25		10–6		10–1		10–5
							10–22	10–19	10–14				10–1		
							10–22	10–19	10–14						
							10–22	10–19	10–14				10–1	10–5	
	10–18		10–8	10–18			10–22	10–19	10–14		10–6		10–1	10–5	10–5
	10–18		10–8	10–18			10–22	10–19	10–14		10–6		10–1	10–5	10–5

The Importance of Classroom and School Culture   6

During the 5 years Ms. Harris had been principal in this school she'd focused on building a constructive school culture. Each day she met staff, students, and parents as they entered the school, offering a smile or a handshake, and getting dozens of hugs each day from the children. She'd worked to build a culture where people felt safe and connected, a place where good learning and problem solving were possible, and a place where fear and distrust did not shut down optimal states of thinking. Sometimes it was difficult, like when last-minute budget cuts and mind-numbing bureaucratic directives added stress and consternation to an already challenging job.

But today was not one of those days. Today she'd started the day early by meeting with three of her strongest teachers, Mrs. Rhodes, Mrs. Peterson, and Mrs. Samuels. Secretly, she'd wondered how long they would work on this project before they'd ask to meet with her and share their ideas. She'd seen them working after school, and heard the occasional remark about the unpaid and unofficial curriculum committee they'd begun. These were real teachers, she thought as she prepared coffee and muffins for the meeting. These were the teachers she'd chosen for her own nephew when he was attending her school.

"We have started to work on something important," began Mrs. Peterson.

"And challenging," interjected Mrs. Rhodes with a smile. "I think this is my first committee in almost 20 years."

"I've been curious," said Ms. Harris.

They showed the principal research summaries from the Casey Foundation and the Foundation for Child Development regarding the importance of early learning success. They discussed the power standards and the Common Core State Standards, and the importance of vigilantly monitoring progress toward crucial outcomes. Mrs. Samuels explained their efforts to focus on a viable literacy curriculum, identify crucial learning outcomes, and then figure out how to monitor progress and adjust instruction to give students enough time and help to achieve all the essential literacy outcomes.

"I thought Ms. Sanchez was working with you," said Ms. Harris.

"She is," answered Mrs. Samuels, "but she wasn't sure if she should come with us today."

"Really?" said Ms. Harris. "Does that mean that because she's young and untenured she wasn't sure if she should come?"

"Probably so," answered Mrs. Rhodes.

"That concerns me," said Ms. Harris. "I want this school to be a safe place to explore good ideas."

"And it is," confirmed Mrs. Samuels. "But she worked in another school before she came here, and there was an angry culture."

The principal nodded and made a note to herself. "I'll talk to her later. Thank you. Now, what can I do to support your work?"

"There is a little more to explain," said Mrs. Peterson. She showed her principal the essential skills she and the kindergarten teacher were aiming to help every child deeply learn this school year. She showed her the baseline data they had collected in kindergarten and first grade.

"You've done a lot of work," Ms. Harris said while poring over the inventories. "And you're designing instruction based on what you know about your students?"

"Exactly," Mrs. Rhodes and Mrs. Peterson said in unison.

"What about covering all the Grade Level Content Expectations?" asked the principal, looking up at the teachers.

"The GLCEs cannot be made into a viable curriculum," Mrs. Rhodes started to protest.

"No kidding. I get it. I've been saying that at curriculum council for years."

"Then why hasn't it changed?" asked Mrs. Rhodes.

"The elephant moves slowly, it seems," answered Principal Harris. "But let's get back to my question. This is exciting work. How can I support you?"

They finished the meeting with an understanding that they would call this a pilot project. The teachers would continue to collect developmental reading assessment (DRA) data at the end of each marking period, and all agreed they were valuable data. The teachers would also continue to use the end-of-marking-period district content test for math, social studies, and science. None of the educators liked this idea because the test served as a pacing guide for curricula that covered way too much content, but everyone acknowledged that it was still required by the district.

Mrs. Peterson hurried to her classroom to be ready to greet students as they arrived. She later remembered that day as the day they were given "pilot project" status, and also as the day that Leroy Brown moved to town and was placed in her first-grade classroom.

Halfway through the morning Ms. Harris walked Leroy to class and introduced him to Mrs. Peterson. For such a young child, Leroy had the most amazing swagger. Other students were drawn to look at him as his teacher showed him the room, assigned him a seat, and then introduced him to his classmates. Looking around the classroom, Leroy settled in with a smile. It was just before lunch when he first tested the limits. He folded up his writing assignment without completing it, put it away into his folder without showing it to the teacher, tossed the folder on the floor, and leaning back in his chair gently rocked on the back legs of the chair with his arms folded authoritatively over his chest.

Noticing his rocking on the chair, Mrs. Peterson came next to him. "Leroy, are you feeling alright?"

"Yep. Just getting hungry. How long before lunch?"

"Oh, Leroy," said Mrs. Peterson with a smile, "this is so sad. In this class we keep all four legs of the chair on the ground, and we wait for my signal before putting work away in the cupboard."

"That's fine," said Leroy. "I'll keep that in mind for tomorrow." He continued to rock back in his chair.

Placing her hand on the back of the chair and firmly holding it in place, the experienced Mrs. Peterson called for the class to clean up and get ready for lunch. When the tables were clean, and all the work had been put away in each student's cupboard, she asked the children to get in line for lunch. Motioning for Leroy to stay in his chair, she asked Marcus to lead the group in a single-file line to the cafeteria. The group exited the room, and the classroom was now quiet, and Mrs. Peterson waited.

"I'm hungry," Leroy said after a moment.

"I know."

"I need my lunch."

"You sure do," Mrs. Peterson agreed.

"Can I go now?" he asked sharply.

Standing next to him, feeling empathy for this strong-willed boy who wants to rule the world, Mrs. Peterson just shook her head. "We'll talk about it just as soon as your voice is soft like mine."

Leroy looked at her. He waited for a few seconds. Then in a soft voice, he said, "I want to go to lunch."

"Thanks for using your kind voice. And I'll be taking you to lunch as soon as I carefully teach you how we sit and how we put away our work."

And then they practiced. Mrs. Peterson showed him correct sitting. Then he showed her back. Mrs. Peterson showed him how to finish his work, call the teacher to check, and then put it away in his cupboard. Then he showed her back.

She took him by the hand, then, and walked him to the cafeteria. She could tell he liked holding her hand. "Today, I'll make extra sure you know how things work in the cafeteria," she promised, "and then you'll know how to do it on your own tomorrow." He held her hand tightly. As they walked down the hallway together, Leroy walked close to his teacher. She could feel him leaning slightly against her as they walked.

Effective teachers take all the time necessary to build a positive classroom culture, which is based on the quality of *relationships* established among students and between the teacher and students, well-established *routines* that help order the class and teach appropriate school behaviors, *teacher skills for behavior management*, and the careful *design of instruction*, which offers students an opportunity for success.

> I've come to a frightening conclusion that I am the decisive element in the classroom. It's my personal approach that creates the climate. It's my daily mood that makes the weather. As a teacher, I possess a tremendous power to make a child's life miserable or joyous. I can be a tool of torture or an instrument of inspiration. I can humiliate or humor, hurt or heal. In all situations, it is my response that decides whether a crisis will be escalated or de-escalated, a child humanized or de-humanized.
>
> Haim Ginott

RELATIONSHIPS

Children work harder for teachers they love and respect, and for teachers who love and respect their students. But not every teacher can be expected to build relationships with students in precisely the same way. Some teachers have an outgoing personality and an outrageous funny sense of humor, while others are more organized and serious by nature. In many ways, this is one of the great opportunities for learning offered by the school experience, learning to build connections to a variety of people with different thinking, learning, and personality styles.

It may be fair to say that teachers should find methods that fit their personalities and styles to build connections and relationships with students. Teachers can do the following:

- Meet students at the door as they come into class.
- Use eye contact and smiles.

- Greet each student by name.
- Learn about student interests.
- Attend student activities outside of school.
- Occasionally join students in the lunchroom.
- Ask questions about extracurricular activities.
- Notice important achievements in and outside of school.
- Find time for one-to-one communication.
- Tell stories that engage student interest.
- Use humor to build connections.
- Use respectful language and hold respectful thoughts for students.

In a meta-analysis of more than 100 studies, Marzano (2003) found that on average, teachers who had high-quality relationships with their students had 31% fewer discipline problems, rule violations, and related problems over a year's time than did teachers who did not have high-quality relationships with their students.

> The quality of teacher–student relationships is the keystone for all other aspects of classroom management.
>
> Marzano and Marzano (2003)

ROUTINES

Students are more successful in classrooms where clear expectations have been defined and in which appropriate behaviors for school success are carefully taught, practiced, and reinforced. Unfortunately some teachers and some school districts have responded to overwhelming content expectations by taking short cuts in the development of classroom procedures and routines. Rather than taking the time needed for the careful development of procedures and routines, these teachers may offer a quick explanation of expectations, maybe even make a bulletin board highlighting desired behaviors, but cannot find the time to carefully teach and practice procedures until they become classroom routines. These teachers are likely to get angry or frustrated when children fail to follow the procedures that were introduced but not carefully taught, and were never learned to the point that they became classroom routines.

Procedures are the steps toward accomplishing a desired school behavior. For example, a procedure for beginning the day may include greeting the teacher at the door, hanging up your coat and backpack, getting your work folder from the cubby, placing the folder on your work table, and then coming to the morning meeting circle and sitting down.

During the first week of school, this procedure is not yet a routine. After modeling, discussing, practicing, and reinforcing the procedures consistently, hopefully it will become a routine before long.

Many children live in families in which routines are well established. In these homes, children will likely have a morning time routine in which they get up, brush their teeth, make their bed, get dressed, have breakfast, help with dishes, check their backpack, and then go to school. There are dinnertime routines, study routines, chores routines, and bedtime routines in these homes. These children usually adapt quickly to school expectations and routines.

Some children do not have the benefit of well-established family routines. Regular bedtimes and mealtimes are not established. Chores and reading time may be inconsistent. These children will need more time to learn and accept the procedures for school behavior. Students may also need to reestablish clear expectations for classroom routines after longer vacation periods, teacher illness (subs sometimes change the routines), and the entry of new students to the classroom group.

Classroom procedures/routines are an essential part of building an environment in which great learning can occur. Depending on grade level, classroom procedures may include the following:

- Beginning the day
- Walking in line
- Getting a drink
- Snack time
- Ways to quiet the classroom
- Handling classroom pets
- Attention signals and quiet signals
- Transitions to another activity
- Lunchroom expectations
- Bathroom policies
- Sharpening pencils
- Lost pencils
- Birthdays
- Asking for help
- Asking someone to play with you
- Forming teams on the playground
- Asking the teacher to reconsider a decision
- Dismissal procedure

Classrooms with well-established procedures for general behavior, seat work, group work, transitions and interruptions, use of material, use of equipment, and the beginning and end of day help create calmer and more orderly environments in which students feel safer and are better able to learn (Bailey, 2001; Emmer, 1984; Evertson & Emmer, 1982). Ideally, the class should establish these rules and procedures through discussion and mutual consent by teacher and students (Glasser, 1969, 1990).

> A well-managed classroom is a task-oriented and predictable environment.
>
> Harry Wong (2009)

TEACHER SKILLS FOR BEHAVIOR MANAGEMENT

Teachers widely report that we are seeing more children coming to school who are skilled at defying adult authority, unaccustomed to persevering at difficult tasks, have difficulty calming themselves, and have not yet learned appropriate social and behavioral skills for school success. Risk factors can include low birth weight, single parent, low socioeconomic status, neurodevelopmental delay, early acting-out behaviors, age of school entry, malnutrition, poor quality of nutrition, inadequate sleep, lack of family routines, prenatal drug exposure, low level of maternal education, adult substance abuse in the home, parental mental health issues, poor parenting practices, abuse in the home, insecure attachment, poor-quality child care or preschool, lack of social interaction, poorly developed oral language skills, time spent with video entertainment systems, and violent media.

Simply put, modern teachers need greater skills for managing behavior than educators from previous generations.

With all the elements of a positive classroom culture, and skills to set firm limits in a loving way, teachers can fortunately cause changes in patterns of behavior that have meaningful long-term results. Even modest gains in teacher-child interactions can produce meaningful skill gains in children (Burchinal et al., 2009). It is widely understood that the trajectory of both academic and behavior learning is established in these early years (Burchinal et al., 2009; Campbell, Pungello, Miller-Johnson, Burchinal, & Ramey, 2001; Schweinhart, Barnes, & Weikart, 1993). This makes the importance of teaching behavioral and social skills essential during the early childhood years, including preschool through grade three.

In the classic *Teaching with Love and Logic: Taking Control of the Classroom*, Jim Fay and Dave Funk (1995) describe nine skills that help teachers set firm limits with anger. These skills include neutralizing student arguing, delayed

> Classroom management skills are of primary importance in determining teaching success. A teacher who is grossly inadequate in classroom management skills is probably not going to accomplish much.
>
> Brophy and Evertson (1976)

consequences, use of empathy and the development of an empathetic class-room, use of a recovery time process to prevent behavior meltdowns, developing positive student–teacher relationships, use of enforceable statements to set limits, choices to prevent power struggles, use of quick interventions to prevent the escalation of behavior, and teaching students to solve problems on their own.

William Glasser emphasizes the need for students to be loved and belong, and describes seven caring habits that teachers should have in the classroom. These habits are part of an emphasis on the development of positive relationship as a precondition for children to understand and take personal responsibility for their choices. The Seven Caring Habits include supporting, encouraging, listening, accepting, trusting, respecting, and negotiating differences (Glasser, 1998).

Nonviolent communication (NVC) is a communication process devel-oped by Marshall Rosenberg and is based on the idea that most humans are innately compassionate, that violence is learned through culture, and disputes are commonly based on misunderstanding someone's attempts to meet basic human needs. A formal NVC conversation follows four steps: making neutral *observations* without judgment, expressing *feelings* honestly and directly, expressing *needs* from a list of fundamental human needs, and making clear, feasible *requests.* Empathy and honest self-expression are the cornerstones of NVC (Rosenberg, 2003).

Conscious Discipline, developed by Becky Bailey, begins by focusing on the educator's self-awareness of attitudes and beliefs that affect student behaviors. It emphases the importance of positive relationships and teaches students to control emotions and to develop social skills and problem-solving skills. Teachers learn to develop procedures for the classroom that help create a respectful community (Bailey, 2001).

The Responsive Classroom is an elementary classroom-management approach developed by the Northeast Foundation for Children. It teaches six tools for classroom management designed to improve behavior and academic outcomes. The tools include using a morning meeting routine to build community, establishing consistent rules and logic consequences, guided discovery of materials that encourage inquiry, academic choice to help children be invested learners, classroom organization strategies, and family communication strategies (Kriete, 2002).

DESIGN OF INSTRUCTION

Children learn at optimal levels when instruction is delivered in a way that allows for understanding and success, mixed with an appropriate degree of challenge. This is the instructional match. A student's prior knowledge, the difficulty of the learning task, the pace of instruction, the duration of the activity, and the student's interest are all factors influencing a child's ability to optimally focus and learn. A match between the child's level of readiness and the instructional task improves on-task behavior, task completion, and task comprehension (Gickling & Armstrong, 1978; Treptow, Burns, & McComas, 2007).

Betts (1946) initially defined the instructional level as a task that is sufficiently familiar yet still provides some degree of challenge to bring about optimal learning for the student. His model described the independent level as too easy for optimal learning and the frustration level as too difficult for optimal learning.

Over time, a mismatch between student skill and the difficulty of the task will create significant problems for any student. Some students may manage frustration better than others for a while, but too much time attempting to learn while in the frustration zone eventually causes all learners, especially young learners, to diminish effort. Some students get frustrated and quit trying, learn to dislike the instructional activity (reading, math, science, etc.) and begin to believe this is something at which they just aren't good. Minimizing instruction that consistently puts children in the frustration zone is essential to avoid turning children into curriculum casualties.

Many teachers describe knowing "the look" of good instructional design. Students are absorbed in the learning activity. Watching a young child happily learning is like watching a master craftsman in action. The child may smile or look serious, might lose all sense of time. There is a positive energy in the room when children are fully engaged in learning.

The basic levels of learning for early reading were specifically described by Gickling and Armstrong (1978), who supported the categorization of levels:

Frustration Level	**Less than 93% sight-word recognition accuracy**
Instructional Level	**93% to 97% accuracy (optimal learning range)**
Independent Level	**98% to 100% sight-word recognition accuracy**

Gickling went on to demonstrate the relationship between instructional level and on-task behaviors, task completion, and comprehension (Gickling & Armstrong, 1978; Gickling & Rosenfield, 1995).

In the development of Reading Recovery, a first-grade reading intervention program, Marie Clay used practice reading at the appropriate instructional level as one of the foundations of successful early reading practice (Pinnel, 1989). The importance of design of instruction at the correct level of challenge is now well accepted as essential best practice.

Allington (2001); Sternberg and Grigorenko (2004); Marzano (2001); Marzano, Pickering, and Pollock (2001); Sornson (2001); Torgesen (2002); Ysseldyke and colleagues (1987), and others include instructional match as a necessary factor for effective instruction and optimal learning.

Fuchs and colleagues (2006) and other researchers have expanded the application of instructional match to learning described as drill tasks, but the levels of challenge that lead to optimal learning have not yet been clearly established. Roberts and Shapiro (1996) found that the 20% unknown to 80% known item condition resulted in a higher percentage of drill tasks learned but resulted in less total material learned compared with more challenging ratios. MacQuarrie, Tucker, Burns, and Hartman (2002) found that drill tasks containing 90% known items led to significantly better retention. Others have suggested the need to individualize the ratio of unknown to known material based on academic area (Cooke & Reichard, 1996; Cooke, Guzaukas, Pressley, & Kerr, 1993). A meta-analysis found that drill ratios containing at least 50% known led to a strong effect, but no specific ratio within that parameter was decisively more effective than the others (Burns, 2004).

> Curriculum functions as a sorting device selectively discriminating between students who succeed and those who fail.
>
> Gickling and Thompson (1985)

Student engagement is crucial for optimal learning (Gettinger & Siebert, 2002). For optimal engagement, it is important to match the level of task difficulty to student readiness and also to make learning relevant to the student's interests and experiences outside the classroom (Gettinger & Siebert; Gickling & Thompson, 1985; Stipek, 1996).

If we wish for every child to have a chance to be a successful lifelong learner, the design of instruction in the early years of learning cannot be used to sort students into winners and losers. Effective teachers take all the time necessary to build a positive classroom culture, which is based on the quality of *relationships* established among students and between the teacher and students, well-established *routines* that help order the class and teach appropriate school behaviors, *teacher skills for behavior management*, and the careful *design of instruction*, which offers students an opportunity for success.

During her years in this school, the principal had worked consciously to build a school culture. At the beginning of every school year she shared a reflection (see Appendix G, Reflection on Classroom Culture) that helped teachers consider the culture they aspired to build in their classrooms. In her second year, as a staff project they developed a set of commitment statements. These were a set of statements about how students would be treated in the school. It took two staff meetings to create a first draft. Then the draft statements were posted in the office and teachers' lounge for

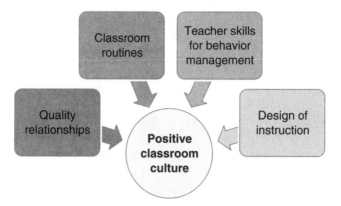

continued study. Not until every teacher had been given extensive opportunity for input did Mrs. Harris ask each teacher to sign the document and post it in her classroom.

OUR COMMITMENTS

In this school, we are committed to ensuring that each student feels physically and emotionally safe and has strong positive relationships with both staff and students. Our school will be a place where students can leave anxiety behind, allowing them to learn optimally. In pursuit of this goal:

- We will greet students daily when they are entering the school and classrooms.
- We will carefully develop and teach classroom and schoolwide procedures, so every student understands how to behave appropriately at school.
- We will explain, rehearse, practice and reteach as many times as needed for students to learn and follow procedures.
- We will ensure students receive instruction at their instructional level.
- We will respond to misbehavior quickly and consistently, with empathy and without anger.
- We will help students develop personal responsibility for their actions.
- Each day we will model empathy, respect, and responsibility.
- We will encourage students to create a powerful belief that they can make a difference in their own lives and in our community.

In her third year as principal, Mrs. Harris asked the staff to work on a set of commitment statements regarding how parents and guardians would be treated in the school. This took some discussion, as there were a few teachers who saw parents as obstacles to a comfortable school culture. With time everyone realized the importance of a positive connection to families, and by going through a similar writing process developed this set of commitments to parents. These were posted outside of every classroom and inside every entry door to the school.

OUR COMMITMENTS

In this school, we will treat parents (and guardians) as welcome and appreciated partners in the education of their sons and daughters. We will help them learn to trust us so that we can work together as a powerful team. In pursuit of this goal:

- We will set aside time each week to communicate with parents/guardians.
- We will communicate through various modes to meet the needs of families.
- We will provide opportunities for parents/guardians to become involved in meaningful school activities.
- We will provide opportunities to discuss a child's needs, progress, and success/achievement within a reasonable timeframe whenever parents/guardians ask.
- We will communicate far more positive information about student progress than negative news.
- We will help families feel a strong positive emotional connection with our school.

In her fourth year as principal, Mrs. Harris took on what she perceived to be the most important single factor in the development of a positive school culture. In retrospect, she wondered if she should have focused her efforts here sooner, since this aspect of culture has the most pervasive effect on the way things get done around the school. She began the discussion by reminding staff of the commitment every one of them had made regarding how children must be treated for them to be optimally ready to learn. Then she reviewed how they had extended that line of thinking to build trust and safety in this school for parents. Finally, she posed the question. If building trust, relationships and clear procedures are crucial for student learning and relationships with parents, is it also fundamental part of a culture in which staff is optimally able to think, learn, collaborate, solve problems? In other words, Mrs. Harris explained, we are going to take a carefully look at building the culture that helps staff thrive and be most effective. For this exercise, every teacher, paraprofessional, custodian, playground supervisor, and cafeteria worker was encouraged to participate.

This work gets personal. If the promise to treat other staff members respectfully was to resemble the other commitment statements, every desire to remember past grudges, form cliques, and selectively treat some staff with disregard would be challenged. It took time. Three staff meetings and 2 months later a final draft emerged. It was a time for thoughtfully considering how to build an interpersonal culture among employees in a public school organization that everyone acknowledged would make teaching more satisfying while improving learning outcomes. By the time the process was complete, every staff member was ready to sign. This commitment to each other remains the heart of the school.

OUR COMMITMENTS

We are committed to creating a culture in which our staff is respectful to each other, supports one another, and appreciates each staff member. We commit to building and maintaining an environment of encouragement, trust, empathy and loyalty towards each other, as we work together to achieve the important goal of academic success for all our students. In pursuit of this goal:

- We will respectfully listen to each other.
- We will build positive relationships so that we can have a safe environment for learning and problem-solving.
- We will work to develop positive communication patterns. We will strive to achieve a six to one (or better) ratio of positive communication.
- We commit ourselves to on-going collaboration with our colleagues.
- We will value honesty between colleagues when discussing professional issues.
- Every issue/problem we deal with will become a chance for us to build professional trust and respect.
- We will treat others as we wish to be treated.

Culture answers the question, "How do things work around here?" Each year when she gave the *Reflection on Classroom Culture* to her teachers, Mrs. Harris pulled out her own reflection. This was her reminder to somehow find time to do the important work in her school (see Appendix G). It was her chance to think about designing opportunities for thinking, learning, and collaborating with her staff.

After Leroy joined her class, Mrs. Peterson set out to review and reestablish every important classroom routine. The introduction of any new element challenges the normal procedural expectations. Every time a teacher is sick for a few days, she must reestablish classroom routines. Every time a school holiday is over, she must restore classroom routines. Every time a human dynamo like Leroy joins the group, every expectation must be reviewed so children know that the rules have not changed.

> The school culture is a complex pattern of norms, attitudes, beliefs, behaviors, values, ceremonies, traditions, and myths that are deeply ingrained in the very core of the organization. It is the historically transmitted pattern of meaning that wields astonishing power in shaping what people think and how they act.
>
> Roland Barth (2002)

Mrs. Peterson was practicing hallway behavior with her class when she felt eyes upon her. Glancing back, she saw Ms. Scott watching her from her classroom doorway. She smiled at the young first grade-teacher with the beautiful dark hair. Usually, Ms. Scott kept to herself, rarely joining the other teachers for after-school activities. Today she stood at the door, started to go back into her classroom, but paused and looked back at Mrs. Peterson.

"Is everything all right?" asked Mrs. Peterson. "Were we too noisy?"

"Oh, no," answered the younger woman. "Mrs. Peterson, do you think we could talk later? I'd like to talk to you if you have time."

"Yes, of course."

Although Ms. Scott had been teaching here for 2 years, she had never before asked her colleague for advice. After school, Mrs. Peterson went into Ms. Scott's classroom.

"I was surprised to see your students practicing hallway behavior," said Ms. Scott. "They already have such respectful behavior in the hall."

"Well, we have a new student who changes the chemistry," smiled Mrs. Peterson.

"Is he trouble?" asked Ms. Scott.

"No. Not trouble. He's wonderful. But Leroy has something like the energy that comes with a big thunderstorm. He makes all the little critters excited. I'm just making sure everyone remembers the class routines."

"Mrs. Peterson," the young teacher began to ask, then looked away.

"What's wrong?" asked the veteran teacher. "Is there a problem?"

"I think I need help," answered Ms. Scott sitting down. She looked shaky. "My class is so hard to control. And we're not beginning to keep up with the content guides. And I know you're busy with your own class and all the other work you do, but I could really use someone to help me. I should be able to handle a first-grade classroom on my own, but really . . ."

She pulled a chair next to the young teacher and sat close. For more than a moment they did not talk. Ms. Scott leaned against Mrs. Peterson and took the older woman's hand.

CHAPTER 6 STUDY QUESTIONS

1. Read and consider the quote from Haim Ginott (see page 56). Is this consistent with your experience?

2. Are teachers in your school taking all the time needed for their students to learn appropriate school behaviors?

3. In your opinion, which of the following factors are not given sufficient time and attention in your classroom? Relationships, routines, teacher skills for behavior management, or instructional design.

4. How would you describe your classroom culture?

5. How would you describe your school culture?

6. What factors make it difficult to build a healthy school culture?

Instructional Support   7

*Responding to Teacher
Requests for Help*

"**C**an you believe I've let that poor girl work just down the hall from me for over 2 years and didn't realize she was struggling? And never really gave her much support?" said Mrs. Peterson at the dinner table with Matt and her husband.

"But you offered, and she said she was doing fine," suggested her husband. "How would you know any different?"

"Is she the cute one with the dark hair?" asked Matt.

Mrs. Peterson shot her son a dark look. "We're talking about a young teacher who has been afraid to ask for help and even in a good school like ours somehow nobody knew how much she was struggling! Can you imagine how hard it must be to be just starting out, trying to cover an overwhelming curriculum, dealing with challenging behaviors, not realizing that everyone needs help sometimes and should be able to get help quickly? And she felt that she somehow needed to handle it all on her own. That's unrealistic. Nobody can do this job without nurturance and support!"

This was a lot more answer than the big blond high school senior had expected. He looked at his dad.

"Yes." Mr. Peterson smiled at his son. "She's the cute one."

At school, Mrs. Peterson discussed it with the principal, Ms. Harris. Both experienced educators felt bad that they had not realized how much the young teacher was stressed.

"She has incredible potential," the principal said about Ms. Scott. "We can't afford to let a person with that much potential become discouraged with teaching."

It was disheartening for the principal. "We've raised the level of trust and respect around this school, but we have a long way to go. I never want a great young teacher like Ms. Scott to feel like she's isolated and unsupported. I just don't think I've done a good job building the expectation of collaboration among the staff."

"You haven't noticed the noncommittee I'm on?" Mrs. Peterson chuckled.

"That group is hardly normal," responded Ms. Harris. "But really, the general perception is that teachers should figure out all the learning and behavioral challenges of increasingly complex children all on their own. We're not well set up for collaboration. We don't prioritize time for collaboration. We don't have staff designated to facilitate collaboration. A teacher could close her door and get minimal observation or adult interaction for years."

"And Ms. Scott does well enough so that we think she's alright, but really she is struggling at school, losing sleep at night, and wondering if she's cut out to be a teacher," added Mrs. Peterson. "I'm just going to have to find time to help her."

"You are already busy with your class," said the principal. "Last time I checked you have your own set of challenges this year."

"She is still an inexperienced teacher, and she's probably afraid to ask the principal for help. I'm guessing she worries that you'll evaluate her poorly if she's not perfect."

"Then let's deal with that misconception as soon as possible," replied Ms. Harris. "We've got to find a way to make professional collaboration the rule rather than the exception. It's not just Ms. Scott. We need a system that encourages staff to reach out and ask for collaboration and support quickly. Not waiting until a problem is huge. If a teacher is struggling to figure out a complex kid, she shouldn't have to do it alone. If she's struggling with a student's chronic behavior problems, there should be help available quickly. If there is a group of children not developing an essential academic skill or behavior skill, it should be expected that we ask for help quickly. Our work is not frivolous. It matters if we do these jobs well."

Like many educators, Ms. Harris had experienced unhealthy school cultures, in which disrespect and the abuse of personal and organizational power were common. Fortunately, she had also worked for Mrs. Gaines as an assistant principal, and in that position saw both the benefits of a positive school culture and all the work that goes into the building of such a culture.

In this elementary school, Ms. Harris wanted to build a culture of *trust*, a culture of *service*, a culture of *continuous learning and improvement*, and a culture of *results*. After more than 4 years of attention to building a positive culture, she knew she was only partway there. Trust was passable within the school but still needed to be better. Building a culture of service was easy in this school because the majority of teachers were zealots for serving the needs of children. A commitment to serving the needs of parents and families was still not well developed. Many teachers were not yet confident in their ability to work with parents, afraid they would not know how to deal with an angry parent or did not have enough expertise or time to serve their needs. Ms. Harris did not yet see her school as a having a culture of continuous learning and improvement or a culture of results. The data sources that schools routinely used were not adequate for a careful monitoring of progress toward important outcomes. The once-a-year state tests changed questions each year and changed cut scores each year. State testing had become a frustrating exercise in chasing a better score using a flawed testing instrument. Without the use of better data sources, it would be hard to ever become a culture of continuous improvement or continuous learning. The principal was quietly excited to see the use of Essential Skills Inventories for ongoing progress monitoring. The actualization of Ms. Harris's vision of a great school culture was still a long way off, but she held on to this clear vision.

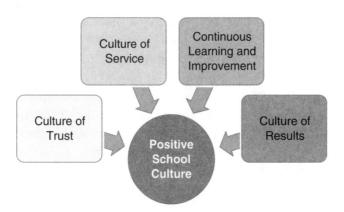

The long-held expectation that teachers should close the classroom door and cover the curriculum is in conflict, both with the hope that all students can become effective learners and the understanding that professional collaboration is an essential part of a learning organization or a high-performing organization. Peter Senge is a primary contributor to the field of organizational learning. According to Senge, learning organizations are those organizations where people continually improve their capacity to create the results they desire and where people are continually learning to improve skills and systems within the organization. He argues that only those organizations that are able to learn and improve will be able to succeed in their field (Senge et al., 2000, 2006).

Although many businesses have made great strides toward becoming learning organizations, schools are known for their incredible ability to resist change and hold onto structures and systems that have been in place since the early 1900s. In schools we give credits based on Carnegie units, which measure seat time. We operate on an agrarian schedule even though we no longer send our children out into the fields to plant and harvest. We send high school students to school earlier than elementary students, even though studies of the alertness rhythms of older students show if they begin school later they will learn better. We teach secondary sciences based on the rule of alphabet (biology, chemistry, and then physics), even though most scientists suggest this sequence is not well aligned to the purpose of developing deep understanding. We offer grades to help compare the learning outcomes of students without being able to know which or whether important skills have been mastered. We spend disproportionately more to educate secondary students than elementary students, without regard for the research that demonstrates the critical importance of the early learning phase. We pay teachers more based on seniority and advanced degrees, neither of which is correlated to better teaching and learning. Because we do.

Business leaders believe that teamwork models are a way to reduce inflexible, bureaucratic mechanisms and increase humanity, collaboration, and creativity (Katzenbach & Smith, 1993; Marchington, 1992). Companies such as Google, Intel, Shell, Boeing, and Apple go to great lengths to structure their workplace environments to empower teams to collaborate. Google has designated a job position called "chief culture officer," and this person's job is to support the collaborative, team-oriented, nontraditional culture of Google (Mills, 2007). According to the Association for Quality and Participation (2008), collaborative problem-solving models in business result in cost savings, improved customer satisfaction, improved product quality, and most importantly, they empower workers to make a meaningful contribution to their company.

Collaborative problem-solving models have been introduced in schools over the years but have not become standard practice in most schools. One of the first was the Teacher Assistance Teams introduced by Chalfont, Pysh, and Moltrie (1979). This teacher support system model was designed to help regular classroom teachers meet the needs of mainstreamed, handicapped children. Although successful in some cases, research showed it was most effective with teachers who held a strong belief in their ability to problem-solve and meet the needs of these children in the classroom (Kruger, 1997). Successive models have included child study teams

(Moore, Fifield, Spira, & Scarlato, 1989), student assistance teams (Aksamit & Rankin, 1993), peer intervention teams (Saver & Downes, 1991), school consultation committee (McGlothlin, 1981) and mainstream assistance teams (Fuchs, Fuchs, & Bahr, 1990).

One of the largest experiments with collaborative problem-solving occurred in Connecticut and Pennsylvania with the implementation of instructional support teams (IST; Kovaleski, Tucker, & Stevens, 1996). The IST model is a three-tiered intervention model that uses classwide interventions, small-group interventions, and individual student interventions to provide the best learning environment possible for each student (Kovaleski & Glew, 2006). Focusing primarily on literacy and numeracy skills, the IST model emphasized the importance of instructional match and the use of curriculum-based assessment. Instructional consultation teams were developed in Maryland as a program designed to improve student performance by improving teacher performance (Rosenfield & Gravois, 1996). The Early Learning Success Initiative (Sornson, 2007) expands on the model of ISTs, emphasizing the importance of developing the whole child, including oral language, literacy, numeracy, motor skills, and social and behavior skills. The ELSI develops a team of responders in the school to support classroom instructional design and emphasizes the use of ongoing formative assessment and responsive instruction to develop essential skills and behaviors during the K–3 years. These models have been shown to reduce referrals to special education and improve measures of academic learning (Kovaleski & Glew, 2006; Newman, 2007; Sornson, Frost, & Burns, 2005).

Much of the impetus to develop these models has come from the desire to help handicapped children be more successful in the regular classroom or to prevent the need for young children to be placed in special education programming. Response to Intervention (RTI) is another such initiative, originally developed in response to the acknowledged flaws of using a discrepancy model to determine which children qualify as learning disabled special education students. The discrepancy model requires that children struggle long enough in early reading or math until they eventually fall one or more standard deviations below their expected level of achievement, as measured by an IQ test. This is often known as the "wait to fail" model. Many authors have criticized the discrepancy model for its unreliability and especially because it causes schools to delay intervention when early intervention might significantly improve learning outcomes and in many cases eliminate the need for expensive and often ineffective special education labeling and services (Hessler, 2001; Sornson, 2001).

RTI is not required by federal law, but rather is allowed as an alternative to the discrepancy model for LD identification. Typically RTI is described as having five essential components, including universal screening of all students to specifically identify learning issues or gaps, quality classroom instruction based on this knowledge of student needs, ongoing monitoring of progress toward critical outcomes, collaboration with colleagues to refine instructional practices in the classroom or identify services outside the classroom, and the provision of additional services (Tier 2) outside the classroom to give additional time or specific instructional strategies. RTI is usually associated with the early intervention and the three-tier model, with Tier 1 describing quality classroom instruction with ongoing progress monitoring, Tier 2 describing additional services provided in addition to the regular classroom instruction, and Tier 3 describing intensive services beyond the second tier, which usually means special education services.

Early-reading expert Richard Allington (2005, 2008) has called RTI "possibly our last, best hope" for achieving full literacy in the United States, but he is also critical of the way it has been conceptualized and implemented in most schools, citing the use of the least experienced staff to work with the neediest students in some districts, the use of packaged one-size-fits-all reading programs, and the use of digital progress monitoring instruments (Rebora, 2010). Since RTI is not a specific program with clear guidelines or standards, it has been implemented in vastly different ways across the country.

For Ms. Harris, developing a system that allowed her staff to work smarter and more collaboratively was a big part of becoming a school with a culture of *continuous learning and improvement* and a culture of *results*. But at times, it was an immense challenge. She worked within a larger system that mandated overwhelming content expectations, complex bureaucratic regulations, and overreliance on simplistic summative assessments. She served increasingly needy students and parents. In most of the district and county meetings she attended, the anxiety was thick. She often found herself coming back to school after these meetings, leaving her lists of things to do in the office, and walking down to the kindergarten classrooms. The open hearts in a kindergarten classroom helped ground her, reminded her why she loved this work, and helped Ms. Harris regain the grit she needed for the work ahead.

The principal wished she had a collaborative instructional support structure already in place. Reluctantly she agreed that for now Mrs. Peterson would find time to support the young first-grade teacher.

Ms. Harris knew her staff needed more than occasional moments of professional support. To improve the collaborative learning and problem-solving culture in her school, she needed a system. The principal looked to one of the better systems thinkers she knew for help. She reached out to the experienced kindergarten teacher with an attitude, the committee avoider, the teacher who loved her classroom and protected her students with the heart of a lioness. With the help of Mrs. Rhodes, Ms. Harris began to construct a plan to encourage collaboration that would improve both staff learning and student results. Both women agreed the system needed to be simple and accessible, respectful of teachers as professionals, focus on viable and measurable results, encourage learning and sharing among staff, and encourage quick and responsive interventions before childhood delays grew too large. But within the context of expected district procedures, this was no small task. They began with an analysis of where there were compared to where they want to be.

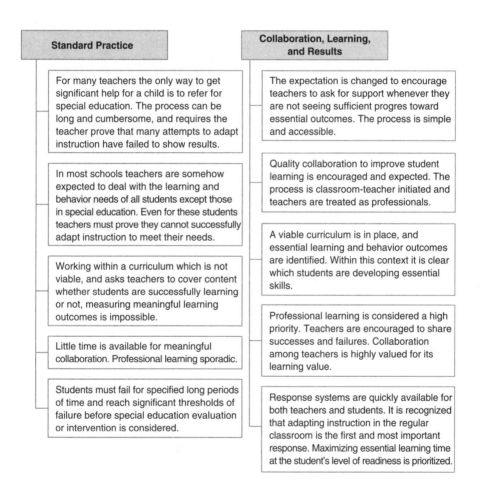

Standard Practice	Collaboration, Learning, and Results
For many teachers the only way to get significant help for a child is to refer for special education. The process can be long and cumbersome, and requires the teacher prove that many attempts to adapt instruction have failed to show results.	The expectation is changed to encourage teachers to ask for support whenever they are not seeing sufficient progres toward essential outcomes. The process is simple and accessible.
In most schools teachers are somehow expected to deal with the learning and behavior needs of all students except those in special education. Even for these students teachers must prove they cannot successfully adapt instruction to meet their needs.	Quality collaboration to improve student learning is encouraged and expected. The process is classroom-teacher initiated and teachers are treated as professionals.
Working within a curriculum which is not viable, and asks teachers to cover content whether students are successfully learning or not, measuring meaningful learning outcomes is impossible.	A viable curriculum is in place, and essential learning and behavior outcomes are identified. Within this context it is clear which students are developing essential skills.
Little time is available for meaningful collaboration. Professional learning sporadic.	Professional learning is considered a high priority. Teachers are encouraged to share successes and failures. Collaboration among teachers is highly valued for its learning value.
Students must fail for specified long periods of time and reach significant thresholds of failure before special education evaluation or intervention is considered.	Response systems are quickly available for both teachers and students. It is recognized that adapting instruction in the regular classroom is the first and most important response. Maximizing essential learning time at the student's level of readiness is prioritized.

Even though there were some decisions over which the staff in this one school had no control (district pacing guide, choice of primary instructional materials, design of state assessment instruments, meager resources for professional development, class size), there were still many steps they could choose to take. Long ago Ms. Harris had learned that it was often easier to ask forgiveness than to get permission, and so they proceeded.

Working with special education and support staff, Ms. Harris identified three teachers who could carve 2 to 3 hours a week out of their busy schedules to serve as grade-level case managers. These teachers would be first responders to teacher requests for support. Their job was to clarify the teacher's request, bring in additional support staff if needed, collaborate with the teacher to develop a plan to work on the teacher's first priority concern, follow up with the teacher if needed to determine if the support is working, collaboratively adapt the plan if necessary, and help monitor progress until success was achieved. Along with the reading teacher, a speech and language teacher, and a special education resource room teacher, Ms. Harris and Mrs. Rhodes developed a one-page form to begin the request process (see Appendix M), and the beginning of their building instructional support procedures. Their guiding principles were posted. The written procedures were distributed and reviewed in grade-level meetings. The conversation had reached another level. It was almost Thanksgiving by the time the school's support team procedures were ready for implementation. It was a beginning.

The Principles of Our Instructional Support Process

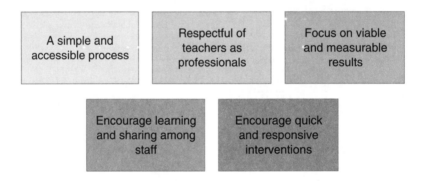

For weeks, Mrs. Peterson had been using prep and after-school time to work with Ms. Scott in her first-grade classroom. After some consideration, their first priority was to develop clearer classroom procedures and help every child learn to use and support them. The young teacher watched her classroom transform as the students practiced their procedures, became more secure in their surroundings, and opened up to the teacher and to each other in a way they could not in their old more chaotic classroom.

"Won't I get behind in the delivery of the content expectations if I give so much time to practicing classroom procedures?" Ms. Scott asked more than once.

But she was reassured by the experienced Mrs. Peterson, and soon the class had settled into a happy rhythm. Only then did Mrs. Peterson consider asking if Ms. Scott was ready to learn to differentiate reading instruction based on the different levels of readiness in her class.

"But there is so much to cover! I can't imagine getting it all covered while allowing some students to work longer at their own skill level!" said the young teacher.

"Yes. I think you are absolutely correct. You can't possibly cover all the GLCEs and also effectively differentiate instruction. So let's talk about which literacy objectives are the most important for all children to learn," replied Mrs. Peterson to the concern that was becoming her passion.

They worked to develop focused lessons, identify which children had already mastered some of the essential skills, and design literacy groups and literacy centers and intensive support for those who needed to catch up to grade-level readiness. Mrs. Peterson showed the younger teacher how to offer activities and challenges for the better readers. Ms. Scott became interested in the varied motor skills of her students, and Mrs. Peterson asked the principal to help identify some parents and grandparents who could become *Motor Moms and Dads* volunteers. By the time Ms. Scott identified Natalie as having serious oral language and motor skill delays that were affecting her progress in reading, the instructional support team system was in place and Mrs. Samulski was ready to serve as case manager.

Instructional Support in Action

- Keep track of the skills and needs of all students by using a simple system of assessment which looks at the devlopment of the whole child.

- Identify each student's specific strengths and needs as soon as possible. Offer responsive instruction, giving students work at the appropriate level of difficulty.

- Intensify instruction for students who do not respond to typical instruction.

- Ask for support if needed.

- Collaborate to determine a student's instructional level and his most important areas of need.

- Get support to deliver the intensive instruction a student needs.

- Keep track of progress.

- Work together in a collaborative process until every student's language, motor, numeracy, literacy, behavior, and social skills have reached proficiency for that grade.

The study group continued to meet twice a week after school and by now more teachers were attending. Mrs. Wheeler, a serious and thoughtful kindergarten teacher, asked to join. Two of the Title I reading support teachers, Mrs. Stanley and Mrs. Whitney, brought their many years of experience to the group. Mrs. Samulski worked in special education and had two young children, but somehow managed to come one day per week. The only male teacher in the building, Mr. Wheaton, asked if he could come on days he was available, and then never missed a meeting. They divided into K–1 and 2–3 working groups. Mostly they focused on essential literacy skills, but Mrs. Peterson and Mrs. Rhodes were using the entire *Essential Skills Inventory* for their classes and before long others were experimenting with the whole-class inventory.

Occasionally, the group encountered research questions they struggled to answer and Mr. Wheaton enjoyed finding primary references and doing a brief lit review. Ms. Scott wanted to better understand why balance and bilateral motor skills impacted readiness for reading. Mrs. Samulski wanted references to successful oral language development programs. Mrs. Jackson wanted to know if behavior and social skills were better predictors of long-term success than standardized state assessment scores. Mrs. Wheeler wanted to know everything she could about effective parent education initiatives.

A few days before Thanksgiving break, Mrs. Peterson asked her husband and son if they'd mind her inviting Ms. Scott to their home for Thanksgiving.

"Her family lives in Minnesota," she explained, "and it's too far to drive for the weekend."

"Is she the cute one?" inquired Matt.

"Yes, but she has a boyfriend," answered his mother.

"Is he coming?"

"Yes, I invited them both," she answered.

Matt looked at his father. "He's not good enough for her," said Matt with a smile.

"I think you are exactly right," said Mr. Peterson.

"There will be no picking on that young man at Thanksgiving," she reproached them softly.

CHAPTER 7 STUDY QUESTIONS

1. Should teachers be encouraged to ask for support when they are struggling to meet the learning needs of a student or group of students?

2. How did standard practice (page 63) develop in American public schools?

3. What would you observe in a school culture that prioritized continuous learning and improvement?

4. What are the major learning initiatives in your school this year?

5. How much of a priority is ongoing professional learning for you?

The Importance of 8
Quality Preschool

Finally, Mrs. Peterson found some time to come down to Mrs. Rhodes's kindergarten classroom. It did not take her long to pick out the child they'd been talking about earlier that morning. David was big for his age, and his body was rigid with effort as he clutched the pencil like a club and tried to draw a picture at the worktable. His hands just would not do what he wanted. He rubbed his eyes and tried again, this time tearing the paper with the force of the pencil. Pushing away from the table, David got up and walked the edges of the room. Two boys were working together at the math center, and David wanted to join them but did not know how to ask. He just stood there waiting and the boys ignored him.

From across the room, Mrs. Rhodes caught her eye and smiled. Next to Mrs. Rhodes, holding on to her pant leg, was Tanya. As Mrs. Rhodes moved through the room giving attention and encouraging good work, Tanya was with her every step of the way. After a moment, Mrs. Rhodes joined Mrs. Peterson.

"Good morning, Tanya," said Mrs. Peterson. But Tanya turned away and put her eyes behind the legs of her kindergarten teacher.

"Can you say good morning to Mrs. Peterson?" encouraged the teacher.

The tiny student smiled lovingly at Mrs. Rhodes. "Yes, ma'am," she replied with a soft voice, but she did not look in the direction of the classroom visitor. She held on tightly to Mrs. Rhodes pants.

"Tanya gets little breaks when she does excellent work," Mrs. Rhodes said in a voice for both the student and her visitor. "She gets to stay with me for a few minutes, and then she heads right back to work."

Getting down to eye level, Mrs. Rhodes said to the little girl, "And now it's time to get back to work. Were you in the reading center?" The dark-haired beauty nodded and headed back to the reading center.

When Tanya was fully engaged in her work, the teachers stepped back to scan the class. David was still standing next to the math center. The boys were engrossed in their activity and had forgotten he was there.

"Some of them come to kindergarten with so few language and motor and social skills," said Mrs. Rhodes. "Almost half my students get free lunch, and with the economy some of the parents are really struggling. If they get preschool or child care at all, it's usually of poor quality. More than half of the children have televisions and game systems in their bedrooms. Only a few have regular bedtimes or reading routines before bedtime."

"Look how happy they are," smiled Mrs. Peterson.

It was true. This was a calm and happy classroom.

"You know you've made my life more difficult," Mrs. Rhodes said quietly, looking at her friend.

"How so?"

"Every day I look at my skills inventory, and every day I know exactly which students already need to make multiple years of learning gains just to be fully ready for first grade. Tanya is smart, but she's hardly ever played with children and has so many social skills to learn. And sweet David, he needs basic language skills, social skills, motor skills, can't begin to hold scissors, and until he came to my class, David had never even touched a crayon."

Even in watching these students for a few minutes, the experienced teachers could recognize patterns of strength and weakness. Building a solid foundation of language, motor skills, behavior and social skills, literacy and numeracy skills for these children is no small challenge. Covering a list of grade-level content expectations is not an option for a teacher devoted to helping these children become ready to succeed. These children need a depth of analysis and understanding that goes way beyond racing through lessons or chapters. They need a teacher who can create a culture of safety and love in which deep awareness of each child guides the teacher as she designs instruction to meet their individual needs.

Shoulder to shoulder, Mrs. Rhodes and Mrs. Peterson stood watching the children.

During the last decade, awareness of the benefits of high-quality early childhood programs has significantly increased. Forty states and the District of Columbia provide some form of publicly funded preK. Enrollment in state-funded preK has grown more than 70% (Barnett et al., 2010). Compared with other nations, however, United States enrollment in preK early education is relatively low. Belgium, France, and Italy enroll 95% of children ages 3 to 6 in universal, public preschool programs. Other countries such as the United Kingdom, Sweden, Hungary, Japan, Germany, Spain, and Russia all have higher percentages of 4-year-olds enrolled in school than the United States does (Organisation for Economic Co-operation and Development, 2010). According to the National Commission on Behavior and Social Sciences and Education, "Children who attend well-planned, high-quality early childhood programs in which curriculum aims are specified and integrated across domains tend to learn more and are better prepared to master the complex demands of formal schooling"(Bowman, Donovan, & Burns, 2001, p. 8).

The benefits of preK are especially potent among children from low-income and minority families. Children living in poverty start kindergarten 12 to 14 months behind their peers in prereading and language skills (Shonkoff & Phillips, 2000). According to 2010 census data, more than one out of every five U.S. children lives in poverty conditions. Minority children show the highest rates, with nearly 40% of African American children and 35% of Hispanic children falling below the poverty line (U.S. Census Bureau, 2011). These children are more likely to struggle in the classroom. Children from poor families are twice as likely to repeat a grade, and they are about 10 times as likely to drop out of high school (Zorn et al., 2004).

In the landmark study by Todd Risley and Betty Hart (1995), researchers recorded language interactions in the homes of young children over a 2½-year period. These families were sorted into three groups based on socioeconomic status: professional class, working class, and poverty. The goal was to discover what was happening in children's early experience that could account for the significant difference in rates of vocabulary growth among 4-year-olds. With a rich data source, the authors were able to analyze differences among the groups. Children in poverty were exposed to approximately 616 spoken words per hour, while children from working class families were being exposed to 1,251 spoken words, and children in professional class families were hearing 2,153 spoken words. The cumulative effects of this rate of exposure to language are considerable.

	Poverty	Working Class	Professional Class
Word exposure by age 4	13 million	26 million	45 million
Ratio of encouragements to discouragements per hour	5 to 11	12 to 7	32 to 5

A difference in the use of encouraging or discouraging words was also noted. The average child in a professional family was experiencing 32 affirmatives and 5 prohibitions per hour, a ratio of 6 encouragements to 1 discouragement. The average child in a working-class family was experiencing 12 affirmatives and 7 prohibitions per hour, a ratio of 2 encouragements to 1 discouragement. The average child in a family on welfare was hearing 5 affirmatives and 11 discouragements per hour, a ratio of 1 encouragement to 2 discouragements (Hart & Risley, 2003). These differences are so significant as to surely be a part of the typically lower levels of language development among poor children upon school entry.

High-quality preK helps to decrease these achievement gaps. In a classic investigation, the High Scope Perry Preschool Study (Weikart, Bond, & McNeil, 1978), participants in a high-quality preschool program were more successful in academics than were participants in the control group by age 19, and they also developed stronger social skills and looked forward to greater economic prospects. By age 27, participants boasted lower arrest rates, higher income levels, and greater rates of high school completion. The benefits only grew as the participants aged, and they compounded by age 40. The researchers estimate that over the course of the participants' lifetimes, every $1 invested in early childhood education programs yielded more than $17 in returns to society (Barnett, 1996; Schweinhart et al., 2005).

The Abecedarian Project was another long-term analysis of quality early childhood interventions. This full-day and year-round program served children from infancy to age 5. The support given was extraordinary. From infancy to age 5 (when public kindergarten began), children attended the program 8 hours a day, 5 days a week, 50 weeks a year. Diapers, food, and transportation to school were provided, along with academic and physical enrichment school activities. A home–school resource teacher served as a liaison and provided parents with individual curriculum to help them work with their children. Half of the children in the preschool program received additional services in the K–3 school years. Relative to their peers in the control group, the program participants were less likely to be retained in grade, less likely to need special education, had better reading scores and math scores, completed more years of school, were more likely to attend college and more likely to be in skilled jobs (Burchinal et al, 1997; Campbell et al., 2001).

Quality early childhood interventions also produce other long-term benefits such as reduced placement in special education (Sornson, 2007; Sornson, Frost, & Burns, 2005), lower grade retention, and higher graduation rates (Hernandez, 2011). James Heckman, a Nobel Laureate in economics, estimates that high-quality early intervention programs produce from $3 to $17 in social benefits for every dollar invested (Heckman & Masterov, 2007). Tim Bartik (2011) describes the many specific economic benefits to society that come from investment in quality early childhood programs.

With the overwhelming data supporting the efficacy of quality early intervention programs, it is consternating to consider the mixed results of investigations into the efficacy of Head Start. Originally developed in 1965 as a summer school preschool program for children in poverty, Head Start was expanded the following year into a year-round program. As of 2011, an estimated 900,000 children are served annually in Head Start.

> If learning begets learning, then interventions at younger ages have great potential to generate cumulative benefits by altering a child's future developmental trajectory.
>
> Karoly, Kilburn, and Cannon (2005)

In 2010, the Head Start Impact Study reported findings from an extensive analysis including nearly 5,000 children. The study examined the examined the cognitive development, social-emotional development, and physical health outcomes of Head Start students as compared with a control group that attended private preschool or stayed home with a caregiver. Key findings from the study include the following:

- Four-year-old children in Head Start for 1 year had improved outcomes on vocabulary, letter-identification, spelling, preacademic skills, color identification, letter naming, and parent-reported literacy interests and skills, compared with the control group that attended a private preschool or stayed with a private caregiver.
- Three-year-old children in Head Start for 2 years had improved outcomes on vocabulary, letter-word identification, preacademic

skills, parent-reported emergent literacy, perceptual motor skills, applied math problems, and some aspects of behavior. There were also measured improvement of some parent behaviors dealing with health issues, spanking, reading to child, and family enrichment activities, compared with the control group.

- The Head Start Impact Study evaluated 41 measures of cognitive development, 40 measures of emotional development, and 10 measures of parent behavior. By the end of first grade, many of the measured gains had faded, and only one cognitive impact was shown for each group. For the 4-year-olds, vocabulary remained improved, and for the 3-year-old cohort, the oral comprehension skills remained improved over the control group.

- By the end of first grade, there was mild evidence that the 3-year-old Head Start group had more positive relationships with parents. For the 4-year-old group, there were improved outcomes on health insurance coverage. For the 3-year-old Head Start group, there were improved parent behaviors related to time out, authoritarian parenting, and spanking. These parent behavior improvements were not noted for the parents of the 4-year-old group (U.S. Department of Health and Human Services, 2010).

- In the Head Start Impact Study, few significant differences were found between the teachers of the Head Start and control group children for any of the teacher qualification measures. There were also few significant differences on measures of teacher beliefs on how children ought to be taught or on any other measures of classroom activities. As the study children came from families eligible for Head Start and thereby living in poverty, all groups attended schools with much higher levels of poverty than schools nationwide (as indicated by proportions of students eligible for free and reduced-price meals) and were in schools with higher proportions of minority students.

The 2010 Head Start Impact Study concludes that

In sum, this report finds that providing access to Head Start has benefits for both 3-year-olds and 4-year-olds in the cognitive, health, and parenting domains, and for 3-year-olds in the social-emotional domain. However, the benefits of access to Head Start at age four are largely absent by 1st grade for the program population as a whole.

Joe Klein, columnist for *Time* magazine, called for the elimination of Head Start (2011). Grover Whitehurst of the Brookings Institute concluded that

> The children in Head Start are overwhelmingly poor and minority. They are at high risk of starting school far behind their more advantaged peers, and falling further behind over time. They tune-out and drop-out at alarming rates. In a world in which nearly everything we value, from a long lifespan to financial wealth to family stability, is associated with educational attainment, these children's lives are in danger. They desperately need a good education. Further, the nation needs for them to succeed in school if it is to achieve its goal of social equity and if it is to complete internationally in a knowledge-based economy. Preschool is where it has to start. . . . Head Start isn't doing the job the families it serves and the nation need. It must be improved. (Whitehurst, 2011, para. 3)

Other authors consider the long-term effects of Head Start, pointing to decreases in incarceration, adult health status, and men's adult wages (Johnson, 2010). Garces, Thomas, and Currie (2002) support the positive effect on incarceration and adult wages. Deming (2009) reports Head Start's effect on a summary index of young adult outcomes is about 80% as large as Perry Preschool's, yet Head Start costs roughly 50% as much per participant. Steve Barnett, director of the National Institute for Early Education Research, posts, "Some other preschool programs have succeeded to a much greater extent, and Head Start can be reshaped to be similarly effective" (2011). He argues that we respond to the disappointing findings of the Head Start Impact Study by reshaping programs using well-established best practice (Barnett, 2011).

Some observe the complex bureaucratic and regulatory nature of Head Start, and question whether a professional learning culture or innovation can thrive in this environment. Bureaucracy notwithstanding, some Head Start programs are much better run than others. While acknowledging that Head Start needs to be reshaped, many educators recognize that the quality of the public and charter schools these children attend after preschool may be a major contributing factor to the fade effect after Head Start.

Sara Mead (2009) from the New America Foundation advocates for a comprehensive reform strategy focusing on preK–Grade 3, emphasizing the importance of high-quality learning experiences that support academics and social and emotional skills. Focusing on proficiency by third grade,

History suggests that efforts confined to a single grade do not lead to lasting change. A well-documented case in point: When policymakers have invested in prekindergarten programs without sustaining quality enhancements throughout the elementary grades, benefits to participants have tended to fade by third grade, if not sooner. This should not be surprising. We do not expect to achieve a healthier population by fortifying only 4-year-olds' meals or adding exercise just for fourth graders. We recognize that serious health problems affecting millions of American children arise over time, and are best prevented or addressed over time with sustained, evidence-based policies and programs.

Successful preK–3 moves beyond the crisis mentality that has repeatedly swung taxpayers' and policymakers' attention from one "problem grade" to another. It calls for a coherent approach designed to sustain high-quality programs and reflects today's best understandings of how children learn in their formative early years.

Rima Shore (2009)

she notes that "Children who cannot read proficiently by the third grade, or who lack solid math and social skills, will struggle to master more demanding academic content in later grades, falling further and further behind. Achievement in third grade is a strong predictor of children's later academic and life outcomes. For this reason, preK–3rd reforms that seek to ensure that all children achieve proficiency by third grade must be the foundation of every state's and school district's long-term strategy to raise student achievement" (p. 1).

The Foundation for Child Development (2008) has developed a series of research and policy briefs supporting quality preK–Grade 3 education based on the understanding that high-quality preK programs can boost later achievement if quality enhancements are carried forward.

In a 2011 special address to the legislature, Michigan Governor Rick Snyder proposed a birth–Grade 3 initiative, noting, "The early development of cognitive skills, emotional well-being, social competence, and robust physical and mental health is the foundation for school success." He went on to explain, "Our goal must be to create a coherent system of health and early learning that aligns, integrates and coordinates Michigan's investments from prenatal to third grade. This will help ensure Michigan has a vibrant economy, a ready work force, a pool of people who demonstrate consistently high educational attainment, and a reputation as one of the best states in the country to raise a child" (Snyder, 2011).

Children need a good beginning, comprised of a safe, stable and nurturing home environment, quality learning experiences in the home, child care, or preschool, which are then integrated and supported by a quality early learning experience in the K–3 years and completes the development of essential skills and behaviors. Anything less puts a child at risk.

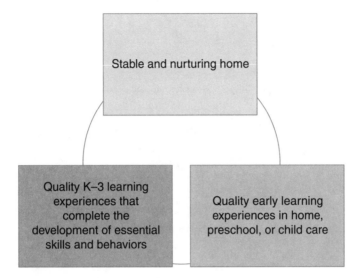

Shoulder to shoulder, Mrs. Rhodes and Mrs. Peterson stood watching the children.

"There was a time I could look at Tanya and David and tell myself they are making great progress. Now with the essential skills in front of me every day, I can measure that progress but I'm more aware of the deficits that will haunt them unless we give them the right instruction and enough time to learn these skills well," Mrs. Rhodes said to her friend.

Mrs. Peterson just nodded.

"I feel the responsibility even more, if you can imagine that," Mrs. Rhodes said with a wistful smile.

"With you, most of them will be in excellent shape to become successful learners," responded Mrs. Peterson.

"Most will," said the kindergarten teacher. "But how about David? Or Tanya? They are just babies. They need so much help and so much more time to learn. They haven't had the advantages of a great start."

"Have you been able to get their parents onboard and helping yet?"

"It took a while, but David's parents are really helping now. They've established a good daily routine, better nutrition, and are reading with him every night before bed. I haven't found a way to connect to Tanya's mom yet," said Mrs. Rhodes.

"Soon. Maybe soon," said Mrs. Peterson.

CHAPTER 8 STUDY QUESTIONS

1. Why are more students coming to kindergarten with delayed development in language, motor skills, and social/behavior skills?

2. What are the benefits of quality preK programs?

3. Do you support continuation of Head Start in its present state? What would you do to improve this program?

4. Has your school district or community begun a discussion of the importance of an integrated approach to quality preK–Grade 3?

5. How would you describe the importance of the early learning years to a citizen without any significant background knowledge in this area?

The Importance of 9
Parent Engagement

For several days in early December, Tyrel was sullen in class. He seemed only to become surlier when Mrs. Peterson asked him what was going on. One day even Jimmy refused to play with him because Tyrel was in such a bad mood. Then as the holidays grew closer, Tyrel's mood shifted and he recovered his happy self again.

With more than 25 years in the classroom, Mrs. Peterson knew that the trajectory of learning was not consistent. For Tyrel, there had been a quick behavior learning curve in the beginning of the school year, and then some regression around Halloween, followed by a steady improvement pattern until early December. Now he seemed to have recovered from the unhappy early December phase, regained his cheerful self, and his desire to learn to behave well in her classroom. His math skills were developing normally, as were his letter recognition and early reading skills. In the last month, the teacher had noticed considerable improvements in his language and vocabulary skills.

On the last day before the holiday vacation, Mrs. Peterson arrived at her classroom early to set up some last-minute preparations for the end-of-day party and to hide a box filled with the small presents and cards she had prepared for each student. She was working at her desk when she noticed a slight man in her doorway. He was standing quietly, watching her as she looked up, and Mrs. Peterson had the impression he was considering whether to come in the door or retreat.

She beckoned him with her hand. "Come in, please."

The man hesitated in her doorway.

"Please," she said kindly as she stepped away from her desk.

"You look busy," he said. The man wore an old tan raincoat, too thin for the weather outside.

Coming to the classroom door, Mrs. Peterson extended her hand and shook his. "You're Tyrel's dad. I can see it in the eyes," she exclaimed.

He smiled when she noticed the similarity.

"I am so glad to meet you," she said, leading him toward a comfortable chair.

"I'm sorry, Mrs. Peterson. I never answered the phone calls you made or the letters you sent at the beginning of the year," he said without looking at her.

She sat down next to him. "It probably seemed like I was pestering you. But I am awfully glad you brought Tyrel to this school and allowed me to be his teacher. He is such a magnificent child, and I hope we can find some time to talk about all that he's learning."

"He sure likes to be in your class," he said rubbing his hands. "But a few weeks ago, I told him we were moving again."

The teacher felt her breathing constrict. *No*, she thought.

Noticing, Tyrel's dad looked up. "But now we're not moving. Tyrel was more upset that I ever saw. At night I found him sitting up by the window, just looking outside at the dark. Now we've decided to stay."

"You're sure? Is everything all right at home?" asked Mrs. Peterson.

He met her eyes. "We've moved a lot. And Tyrel's mother isn't with us anymore. And after she left I've been sometimes drinking too much. But Tyrel is happy here, and we're staying. And I thought you ought to know."

Hurried family lifestyles and anxious school cultures make it possible for us to forget the importance of building strong reciprocal relationships of support between schools, individual families, and communities. Research has shown that engaging families in the academic life of their children is the one of the best predictors of academic success (Finn, 1998). For students, the benefits of family involvement in their schools result in higher test scores, better attendance, greater graduation rates, and increased college attendance. Benefits also include a report of more positive attitudes, greater motivation, higher self-esteem, less disciplinary problems, and lower rates of high-risk behaviors (Henderson & Berla, 1994). A home environment that encourages learning is more important to student achievement than the family's income, education level, or cultural background (Henderson & Berla).

> When parents are involved in their children's education at home, they do better in school. And when parents are involved in school, children go farther in school and the schools they go to are better.
>
> Henderson and Berla (1994)

For teachers, positive home-school connections create higher teacher morale and greater job satisfaction. For parents, this connection generates more confidence from parents in their decision-making abilities, it empowers parents to develop greater skill in accessing community resources, and it helps build more confidence in helping children with their homework (Henderson & Berla, 1994). Schools that foster healthy connections with the community report better overall achievement and better reputations (Zygmunt-Fillwalk, 2006).

Success in school can be linked to attendance patterns, making reading material available in the home, reading to children, and listening to them read (Lee & Croninger, 1994; Ramey & Ramey, 1999), limiting television and entertainment devices (Kellaghan, Sloane, Alvarez, & Bloom, 1993; Ramey & Ramey), and having family routines including chores for the family (Baker & Sodden, 1997; de Bruyn, Deković, & Meijnen, 2003; Ramey & Ramey; Seligman, 2004).

The Chicago Child-Parent Center (CPC) Program is a federally funded school-based preschool and early school-age intervention initiative for low-income children that emphasizes parent involvement and the development of literacy skills. Each CPC is run by a head teacher and includes a staffed parent resource room, school–community outreach activities, and health services. After preschool and kindergarten, the school-age program in the elementary school provides reduced class sizes, teacher aides for each class, continued parent involvement activities, and an enriched classroom environment for developing reading and math skills.

> Kids who are used to doing chores at home . . . without reminders, without pay, and without arguing . . . are far more respectful and motivated at school.
>
> Charles Fay (2008)

In a 2001 cost-effectiveness study sponsored by the National Institute of Child Health and Human Development (Reynolds, Temple, Robertson, & Mann, 2001), the CPC program was estimated to have produced public benefits for the 1,000 study children in the preschool program totaling $26 million. Relative to the comparison group, CPC preschool participants had a 29% higher rate of high school completion, a 33% lower rate of juvenile arrest, a 42% reduction in arrest for a violent offense, a 41% reduction in special education placement, a 40% reduction in the rate of grade retention, and a 51% reduction in child maltreatment. School-age participation and extended program participation for 4 to 6 years were associated with 30% to 40% lower rates of grade retention and special education placement. Compared to children with 1 to 3 years of participation, extended program participants also had higher achievement test scores in adolescence and lower rates of child maltreatment by age 17. Since 100,000 children have been served by the program to date, these benefits translate to as much as $2.6 billion in public savings since the program opened in 1967.

The Harlem Children's Zone (HCZ) serves poverty-stricken children and families living in Harlem and provides parenting workshops in their

Baby College focused on the needs of children ages 0 to 3, a preschool program, three public charter schools, and child-oriented health programs. Founded by Geoffrey Canada, the HCZ is aimed at breaking the cycle of generational poverty for the thousands of children and families it serves (Tough, 2008).

Starfish Family Services in Inkster, Michigan, provides comprehensive family services including the Parent Empowerment Program (PEP). Aimed at parents with children ages 2 to 10, the PEP is a parent education program that focuses on building family routines, developing emotional control, developing language and literacy, setting limits on behavior in the home, developing motor skills, teaching children to learn through their mistakes, developing numeracy skills, and family routines that support emotional health, physical health, and build networks of support for the family (Sornson, 2012).

At the heart of any successful parent engagement initiative is the ability to build trust. Many parents do not have a positive emotional connection to the educators in their children's schools. They may have had a bad experience with schools in their own lives, or a bad experience with a teacher or principal, or simply heard a story about how some local educator was unfair when dealing with a student or family. Bad news is powerful. It lingers.

Teachers sometimes complain that parents fail to have regular bedtime routines or choose nourishing meals for their children, allow back talk, let kids watch too many or inappropriate games and shows, fail to get children to exercise, and don't spend enough time in conversation and play. In many cases, these complaints are accurate. But many parents lack a strong network of support to keep them on track, teach them what they need to know as a parent, and support them when things get tough.

Without trust and connection, teachers and parents will never have the opportunity for deep conversations about how to support the development of young children. Without trust and connection, parents will not choose to come to the school for information, books, or training on important topics. Without trust and connection, busy parents will stay away from school or engage to the least degree possible. In schools where teachers and principals are plagued with the duties of covering overwhelming content objectives, disciplining defiant children, and responding to mind-numbing bureaucratic demands, finding the time and energy to build connections seems impossible. And yet failing to proactively build trust, build relationship, and create learning opportunities with parents makes the job of teaching infinitely harder in the long run.

How and Tschannen-Moran (2003) defined the five elements on which people base their trust judgments.

1. Benevolence: Does the other care about what happens to you? Are you sure the other will not exploit or take advantage?
2. Honesty: Is the trusted person's character sufficient for your trust?
3. Openness: Will important information be openly shared? Does the other trust you?
4. Reliability: Is the other's behavior consistent? Does this person inspire confidence?
5. Competency: Can the other perform as expected? Follow up on a promise?

Proactive teachers build trust and connection by

- sending letters of introduction before school.
- asking for information about students strengths and needs from parents.
- inviting parents to special events.
- listening more than talking.
- inviting parents to volunteer for meaningful activities.
- regularly contacting parents with good news by phone, mail, or e-mail.
- offering quick response to parent questions and concerns.
- sending classroom newsletters filled with positive stories and pictures.
- avoiding educational jargon.
- show parents how to help their students be successful.
- creating a welcoming environment for conferences.
- listening more.
- offering ideas or advice only after parents are in a calm problem-solving state of mind.
- developing a parent resource library in the classroom or school.
- committing to creating positive emotional experiences for parents when they interact with school.

Over the years, Mrs. Peterson had received many holiday gifts. She'd received cookies and coffee mugs, perfumes and powders, and pens and stationery. Once she even received a racy little halter top. This year was special because Tyrel would be staying in her class. At the end of the day, the first-grade teacher hugged every child and counted her blessings.

In January, the Parent Empowerment Program began, two Saturday mornings per month with breakfast and child care provided, nine sessions in total. Tyrel's dad had signed up but his car was in the shop, and he regretfully called to tell Mrs. Peterson he would not be able to go to the first session. No problem, she'd explained. She'd send a ride.

At 7:30 a.m. on Saturday, Mr. Peterson arrived with two hot cups of coffee. Tyrel's dad was waiting on the porch and quickly got into the car. The men introduced themselves.

"Do you get volunteered for this kind of thing often?" asked Tyrel's dad.

"I should write a book about the things for which I've been volunteered." Mr. Peterson laughed.

When they arrived at school, Mr. Peterson parked the car and got out.

"You're coming in?" asked Tyrel's dad with surprise.

"Yeah. I hear it's worthwhile, and I might learn a thing or two."

"But your son is grown."

"Maybe grandkids someday. Hopefully not soon," said Mr. Peterson. "And my wife says we need more men who stand up for good parenting." He looked at Tyrel's dad and whacked him on the shoulder. "Thanks for being one of those."

CHAPTER 9 STUDY QUESTIONS

1. Does your school have a parent engagement plan?

2. Why do children do better academically and behaviorally when parents are engaged with the school?

3. What are the barriers to parent engagement?

4. What would you love parents in your community to learn?

5. What is your personal plan to build trust and relationship with parents?

When Good People Work Within Lousy Systems

10

In another school not far from here, a different story is unfolding.

On the first day of school in Mrs. O'Connor's classroom, 28 first-grade students found their seats. What the students did not know, and what Mrs. O'Connor could not allow herself to acknowledge, is that she was about to begin the systematic destruction of the academic and social learning future of several of these children.

As an experienced teacher, Mrs. O'Connor was already feeling the pressure. Her school had been sanctioned for failing to demonstrate adequate yearly progress, based on the reading and math scores of students in the upper elementary grades on state-mandated tests. Everyone was anxious to achieve higher scores. Her district's response included a revision of the literacy curriculum to include a scripted phonics program, rigid pacing guides for all learning subjects, less time for recess, reduced physical education and art, and the elimination of music class. They changed to a new math program that moves through content at an amazingly fast pace. *Spiraling*, Mrs. O'Connor was told reassuringly when she asked if all children were ready for this pace.

In her first years as a teacher more than two decades ago, Mrs. O'Connor would spend much of the first few weeks of school, and hours every week throughout the year, working hard to develop a caring classroom culture, getting to know the students, teaching simple and eventually more complex procedures for classroom behavior. But recently she'd been criticized for giving time to these purposes. In her evaluations, it was said that she was not demonstrating academic rigor. The time

> If children don't understand the content, don't worry. Keep teaching. The curriculum will spiral around to the missing math concept at some point in the future.

demands of teaching the state-mandated 278 first-grade content expectations allow little time for developing culture and relationships. The content expectations cannot wait.

Within the first week of school, Mrs. O'Connor had an impression of the varied learning needs of her students. Alexandra and Rachel were bright eyed and chatty. Having observed them briefly, Mrs. O'Connor already knew that their language skills, gross motor skills, visual motor skills, and phonologic skills were in great shape. Sitting behind them were Catherine and Tamika, looking anxious and quiet. They hardly said a word in the classroom. Across the room she sat William and Samuel. They wiggled and fidgeted, and Samuel fell out of his seat several times on the first day of school. From the records, she knew that these boys had struggled in kindergarten. They were premature, low-birth-weight boys with language delays, motor skill delays, poor listening skills, challenging behaviors, and poor social skills who did not know how to recognize all of their uppercase or lowercase letters by the end of last school year.

Back in the 1930s, 1940s, and 1950s, it may have been reasonable to teach in ways that allowed some children to have successful learning experiences and others not. Those students who did not experience academic success, whether based on academic talent, learning experiences in the home, or individual rates of development, eventually became frustrated and dropped out. At a time when good jobs were available for anyone with a good work ethic or a strong back, dropping out of school did not compromise the opportunity to earn a living, support a family, and build a life. Today, things are different.

As instruction began, it was quickly apparent to Mrs. O'Connor that some children were more prepared for the rigors of first grade than others. Cassandra and Rachel quickly grasped the classroom routines while others did not. Alexandra and Rachel recognized enough sight-words to read independently while William and Samuel did not yet recognize all the letters. Some children understood basic math concepts while others could not count past 10. Some of her students could skip gracefully, balance with eyes closed, hold a pencil and draw with skill, sound out words, make rhymes, remember three-step oral directions, respect classroom procedures, and delay gratification. Others could not.

By the end of September, Mrs. O'Connor clearly recognized that Monica, Robert, Samuel, William, Theresa, and several others did not understand basic number concepts. Their counting skills were erratic. They did not quickly recognize sets of three, four, or five on a counting frame, or with any other manipulative. They did not understand how to count on from a number, that is, 5 plus 2 more gives you 5, 6, 7! They did not understand the value of basic numbers, but the curriculum called for them to be doing worksheets that assume basic number concepts are already well understood. The curriculum train moved on. There was no design or time to go back and teach these basic concepts.

Mrs. O'Connor worried especially about her children with language delays. Catherine and Tamika didn't have the oral language skills or the listening skills expected by this age. Often they looked confused. Sometimes they got frustrated when they couldn't find the right words, but mostly they retreated into silence within the classroom. This experienced first-grade teacher knew how to help young children develop language skills, but that time was not allowed within her curriculum plan. Time for singing, conversation within play, and imaginative play was not available.

Mrs. O'Connor knows it is wrong. She knows that Samuel and William need lots more time given to social skill training. She knows that Monica cannot understand the math she is given. It breaks her heart to see Tamika struggle to recognize enough words so she can experience reading fluency and comprehension. Nonetheless, Mrs. O'Connor feels compelled to move forward, ever more quickly forward, toward covering all the required content. Sometimes she explains to parents that she is doing her best to keep up with the pacing expectations of the district, which are based on the testing standards of the state, which are required by the federal government. Mrs. O'Connor does not believe she has the ability to influence the standards and procedures she is expected to follow.

In 1961, Yale University psychologist Dr. Stanley Milgram conducted a now-famous study in which he tried to understand what kind of people he could get to do what they believed was causing great harm to another human. He ran an ad in the New Haven newspaper asking people to take part in an experiment that would last 1 hour and for which they would be paid $4.50. While waiting for their turn, subjects would chat with another participant about the upcoming job. This other person was actually a confederate of the research team. Next, a scientist in a lab jacket would appear and ask each subject to draw a slip of paper out of a hat to determine who would be the "teacher" and who would be the "learner." The research subject always got the role of teacher.

In the presence of the subject, the scientist would then strap electrodes onto the confederate, then move to an adjoining room where there was a machine that was said to deliver electronic shocks to the confederate. The stated goal of the experiment was to measure the impact of negative reinforcement on learning. A word pair memory activity was used. Each time the learner gave a wrong answer, a "shock" was administered by the subject. With each wrong answer, the "voltage" was increased. With the first shock came a grunt. With the second shock came a mild protest. Next, stronger protests. Then screaming and shouting. Then screaming and banging on the walls. Then, when the voltage levels indicated more than 315 volts, the subject would hear nothing but silence. Of course, there were no real shocks being administered to the confederate, but the subject believed them to be real.

Milgram asked social psychologists to predict the results of this study. They predicted that only 1.2 % of subjects would give the maximum voltage. As it turned out, 65% did (Milgram, 1963, 1974).

Mrs. O'Connor has devoted her life to loving, nurturing, and educating children. But somehow she has also passively accepted teaching methods and standards that cause harm to children in ways that can last a lifetime.

We know that children learn best when given time on task at the correct instructional match. Common sense tells us that too much failure causes children to shut down and stop trying. But somehow, in our well-intentioned efforts to "raise the bar" and teach more to our children, we have managed to ignore the readiness issues and the individual differences children bring with them to school. In most schools, we fail to carefully assess each child to see what she knows and what she is ready to learn. We fail to commit to identifying essential skills and then delivering instruction in a way that causes children to experience the greatest learning with the greatest joy.

Instead, we have told our teachers to hit the ground running. Teach more, teach faster, and teach harder. Introduce skills and ideas, hope the students grasp them, and move on. Keep up with the script and the pacing guide. Don't bother to take time to build relationships and routines within the classroom. Cover more content without careful ongoing attention to the quality of learning. It is likely that there will be a time in our future when we look back at this phase of American educational history and think of it as barbaric. Wikipedia may report that

After the beginning of the information age and the knowledge-based economy, American schools clung to the old sort-and-select educational model, and vastly increased the content they hoped children would learn without reconsidering the resources and teaching models needed to help every child have a real chance to build a solid foundation based on early learning success. For many decades in our American schools, we allowed slower developing or less fortunate children to experience frustration and failure. For these children, this led to a significantly less joyous and successful learning experience in the early years of school, which led to less successful learning experiences throughout life. We watched as these frustrated children disengaged from learning, sometimes behaved badly, and often dropped out of school. In our effort to accelerate the pace of learning in our schools, we managed to ignore the need to match instruction to the learning readiness of children. This drained the levels of joy and success for many children at all levels of academic readiness. All this occurred during the age in which lifelong learning became an essential ingredient for personal, social, and economic success.

CHAPTER 10 STUDY QUESTIONS

1. How long must a child experience significant learning frustration before beginning to disengage from the process of learning?

2. In your school, are there scripted learning programs or rigid pacing guides or rigid testing schedules that pressure teachers to push children too fast?

3. Is it difficult for many early childhood educators to challenge the rules of the school system, even if they believe that some practices are not in the best interest of their students?

4. How could you begin a deeper conversation about early learning best practices in your school or district?

Pathfinders   **11**

Three importance of quality learning experiences for young children is not a new idea. Mothers and fathers have known by instinct the significance of the early childhood years. Communities have gathered to ensure safety and learning. Teachers have treated these learning years with skill and reverence. Still, in recent decades, some pathfinders stand out as deeply understanding the importance of early learning success and acting on this knowledge to create ideas, programs, and initiatives that give vision and vigor to those of us who follow in their footsteps.

Each of these pathfinders offered bold leadership in a way that was not easy or popular in their time and circumstance. Since the import of becoming a lifelong learner has never been greater than now, men and women of our generation can honor the pathfinders by building schools and communities in which all our children are given the opportunity to become successful learners and people. These are individuals (mostly) who believed in the importance of early childhood learning success, talked about the importance of early childhood learning success, and then walked the talk.

DAVID P. WEIKART

In the early 1960s, we had not yet entered the information age or experienced the technology revolution. Few were clamoring for school reform and fewer still were urging us to consider the connection between early learning success and lifelong achievement.

Dave Weikart was born into a family of educators in 1931. After serving as a Marine, he taught high school English and biology in Canfield, Ohio, and later began working as a school psychologist for Ypsilanti Public Schools in Michigan. As Director of Special Services in 1962, Weikart collaborated with colleagues to create the Perry Preschool Project. The Perry Preschool Project was designed to find causes and interventions for academic underperformance among students in Ypsilanti's poorest neighborhoods. They developed a program that emphasized active learning and the development of the whole child, which is now known as the High-Scope curriculum.

Recognizing the need for quality research as well as quality programming, Weikart initiated an investigation into the effectiveness of the program. He began a randomized controlled trial of 123 low-income children to examine the long-term effectiveness of the program (Weikart, Bond, & McNeil, 1978). Subjects were followed for decades. Participants in the high-quality preschool program were more successful in academics than the control group by age 19, and they also developed stronger social skills and looked forward to greater economic prospects. By age 27, participants boasted lower arrest rates, higher income levels, and greater rates of high school completion. The benefits only grew as the participants aged, and they compounded by age 40. Researchers estimate that over the course of the participants' lifetimes every $1 invested in early childhood education programs yielded more than $17 in returns to society (Barnett, 1996; Schweinhart et al., 2005).

Weikart was one of the first to recognize the learning disadvantages that come from poverty, the need to address learning needs early on in the life of a child, and the social and economic benefits of early learning success. Data from the Perry Preschool Project were influential to the expansion of Head Start in the late 1960s. In 1970, Weikart left the school district to establish the HighScope Educational Research Foundation. He and his wife Phyllis developed the HighScope Camp, a summer camp for low-income students. Weikart was the author of numerous books and articles about early childhood. The HighScope Foundation curriculum, instructional materials, and training programs are used in nations around the world.

He died December 9, 2003.

CRAIG RAMEY

Craig Ramey directed the 30-year Abecedarian Project at the University of North Carolina, a randomized controlled trial analysis of quality early childhood interventions. The participants in this experiment were 111 high-risk infants born between 1972 and 1977. This full-day and year-round program served children from infancy to age 5. The support given was extraordinary. From infancy to age 5 (when public kindergarten began), children attended the program 8 hours a day, 5 days a week, 50 weeks a year. Diapers, food, and transportation to school were provided, along with academic and physical enrichment school activities. A home-school resource teacher served as a liaison and provided parents with individual curriculum to help them work with their children. Half of the children in the preschool program received additional services in the K–3 school years. The control group was provided with nutritional supplements, social services, and health care to ensure that these factors did not affect the outcomes of the experiment.

Relative to their peers in the control group, the program participants were less likely to be retained in grade, less likely to need special education, had better reading scores and math scores, completed more years of school, were more likely to attend college, and more likely to be in skilled jobs (Burchinal, Campbell, Bryant, Wasik, & Ramey, 1997; Campbell, Pungello, Miller-Johnson, Burchinal, & Ramey 2001).

Ramey's research added to the solid research supporting the cost-benefits and social benefits of a quality home, preschool, and early elementary learning experience. Ramey and his wife Sharon were founding codirectors of the Civitan International Research Center at the University of Alabama at Birmingham. Craig and Sharon Ramey have published almost 500 scientific manuscripts and many books, including several on early child brain and behavior development, including *Right From Birth* and *Going to School.*

MILDRED WINTER

Mildred Winter changed the history of parent learning. As a kindergarten teacher, she recognized the striking disparities in readiness for school among her students. As Missouri's first director of early childhood education from 1972 to 1984, Winter helped raise awareness of the importance of the early years of learning, and especially that learning that occurs in the home. Seeing families without good information regarding child development and without strong networks of support, Winter championed passage of the Early Childhood Development Act, which was approved by the Missouri Legislature in 1984. This act approved implementation of the Parents as Teachers (PAT) program in every school district in the state.

Since its inception in Missouri, PAT has grown to include more than 3,000 programs in all 50 states and six foreign countries. It focuses on families from pregnancy until kindergarten entry and uses trained parents as providers of service in the homes of young families. Independent evaluations of the PAT program show that children in PAT at age 3 are significantly more advanced in language, social development, problem solving and other cognitive abilities, than comparison children. PAT children score higher on kindergarten readiness tests and on standardized measures of achievement in early grades. Parents in PAT are more involved in their children's schooling, read more to their children, and are more confident in their parenting role (Newhill, 1992; Wagner & Clayton, 2001).

Winter demonstrated that trained parents, not social workers or certified teachers, could become effective home visitors, teaching families to effectively improve home routines, language development, behavior, motor skills, and social skills. Now in retirement, Mildred Winter continues as a consultant to the Parents as Teachers National Center in St. Louis.

ROBERT SLAVIN

Bob Slavin is Director of the Center for Research and Reform in Education at Johns Hopkins University, Director of the Institute for Effective Education at the University of York, and the cofounder and Chairman of the Success for All Foundation. His article "Preventing Early School Failure: What Works?" (Slavin, Karweit, & Wasik, 1992) described a metaphoric town in which children were dying of typhoid and other diseases because of contaminated drinking water. Millions were being spent treating victims, but the town council would not build a water treatment plant to prevent the diseases and suffering. Slavin's voice was a clarion call for preventing early learning failure rather than waiting and responding to significant learning issues after years of struggle.

As principal researcher at the Center for Social Organization of Schools (CSOS) at Johns Hopkins University, Slavin began researching the elements of Success for All as part of a partnership with the Baltimore City Public Schools. Success for All's expansion prompted Slavin in 1998 to spin off the program from CSOS. He created the nonprofit Success for All Foundation, which is led by research scientist Nancy Madden.

Success for All is based on the beliefs that

- every child can learn;
- success in the early grades is critical for future success in school;

- learning deficits can be prevented through intervention in pre-school and the early grades, improved curriculum and instruction, individual attention, and support to families; and
- effective school reform programs are both comprehensive and intensive.

Implementation of the Success for All model requires a 3-year implementation process that includes teacher training in a new literacy curriculum, use of language development kits, a daily 90-minute reading period, half-day preschool, full-day kindergarten, tutors, 8-week reading assessments, and family support teams. Some teachers complain about the Success for All's "teacher-proof" curriculum, a strictly organized set of teaching materials. Research regarding the efficacy of Success for All has looked at K–2 implementation only and is the subject of some debate. It is generally agreed that Success for All has the most positive effect on the most at-risk learners in literacy, with higher scores shown in passage comprehension, word identification, and word attack skills. Success for All is currently used by 1,000 predominately low-income schools nationwide.

There is no debate that Robert Slavin helped change the conversation about school reform and helped create a far greater awareness of the need to intervene effectively during the crucial early learning years.

GEOFFREY CANADA

Raised by his mother in the South Bronx in the late 1950s and 1960s, Geoffrey Canada was exposed to the crime and chaos of the streets. In his mid-teens he was sent to live with grandparents in Long Island and won a scholarship and attended Bowdoin College and later Harvard University. His powerful first book, *Fist Stick Knife Gun: A Personal History of Violence in America,* was released in 1995. In this book, Canada recounts his exposure to violence during his childhood and details the escalation of violence that came with new waves of drugs and criminality.

In 1990, he began working with the Rheedlen Centers for Children and Families. In the late 1990s, Canada transformed this agency into the Harlem Children's Zone, committed to breaking the cycle of generational poverty for the thousands of children and families it serves (Tough, 2008). It now serves a 100-block area in Harlem and provides parenting workshops in its Baby College focused on the needs of children ages 0 to 3, a preschool program, three public charter schools, and child-oriented health programs.

Canada is an articulate advocate for changing the lives of children and families through quality education and family support services. His inclusion of parent training, family support, preschool, and school-aged services follows the success of models like the Abecedarian Project. Canada's work has been profiled on *Oprah*, *60 Minutes*, and *Waiting for Superman*. In 2008, Paul Tough published a book titled *Whatever It Takes: Geoffrey Canada's Quest to Change Harlem and America*.

DAVID LAWRENCE JR.

For most of his adult life, David Lawrence was in the newspaper business. He worked as a reporter and/or editor with four newspapers, as editor of the *Charlotte Observer*, publisher and executive editor of the *Detroit Free Press*, and then publisher of the *Miami Herald*, during which time the paper won five Pulitzer Prizes. Dave grew up on a chicken farm in upstate New York, one of nine children. When the chicken farm was close to bust, his family moved to Florida. In the Lawrence family, education was valued. Every sibling graduated from Florida or Florida State, and six of his siblings became teachers.

In 1996, the governor of Florida asked him to serve on a Commission on Education, and somehow he was "hornswoggled" into chairing the task force on school readiness. What he learned led him to retire in 1999 so he could devote all his time and energies to see what difference could be made so children would have a better chance to be successful in school and in life.

Dave Lawrence became president of The Early Childhood Initiative Foundation and the University Scholar for Early Childhood Development and Readiness at the University of Florida. He has served on a variety of blue ribbon panels and committees. In 2002, he led the campaign for The Children's Trust, a dedicated source of early intervention and prevention funding for children in Miami-Dade, which was passed by voters and reaffirmed in 2008 with 85% support. In the same year, he was a key figure in passing a statewide constitutional amendment to provide preK for all 4-year-olds in Florida. In 2009, he helped establish The Children's Movement of Florida, which is a nonpartisan effort to educate political, business, and civic leaders, and all parents of the state, about the urgent need to substantially improve the way we care for our children.

In Dave Lawrence's words,

The greatest American "invention" was not the lightbulb or the telephone or even the Internet. It was the public school. Public school gave our country an abundance of smart and skilled people able to invent and innovate, compete, and prosper—and able to hope and able to lead. High-quality public school, built upon democracy, has been the single most important ingredient to the continuing success of the United States of America.

If we want safe and secure neighborhoods, if we want less crime, if we want more people to grow up to own homes and cars, and more people to share the basic costs of societal well-being, then we must act upon the extraordinary evidence of the power of early investment and the power to grow children who dream and have a real chance to achieve those dreams.

In a state of wisdom, in a country of wisdom, children would be the highest priority of elected leaders—higher than roads, higher than prisons, higher than anything. Why should we settle for anything less than affordable, high-quality basics for all children? Why would we not want this for all children? This is simply the American dream. (Early Childhood Initiative Foundation, 2011)

JAMES HECKMAN

James Heckman is a Nobel Prize Laureate in Economics, the Henry Schultz Distinguished Service Professor of Economics at the University of Chicago, and Professor of Science and Society at University College Dublin. Heckman has published more than 270 articles and several books, and has received numerous awards for his work. In recent years, Heckman has focused his work on inequality, human development and life cycle skill formation, with a special emphasis on the economics of early childhood. In doing so, he has become one of the strongest voices for the economic benefits to society of intervening early in the life of a child.

In a 2011 letter to the Joint Select Committee on Deficit Reduction, he summarized important points from his research:

Deficits in skills in early childhood are perpetuated and magnified throughout life. Current policies fail to properly recognize the life cycle dynamics of skill formation. The United States invests relatively little at the starting point—in early childhood development—and as a consequence pays dearly for this neglect at every point thereafter. Our country will be unable to compete in the global economy if it does not address the increasing numbers of children who are not prepared for success in school, career and life.

Investments in quality early childhood development more than pay for themselves. Concern over the costs of early childhood development programs is warranted, but should quickly evaporate when they are balanced with their returns. Quality programs such as the Perry Preschool Program cost close to the amount spent per child annually in secondary education in public schools. Yet, the rate of return for investment in quality early childhood education is 7–10% per annum through better outcomes in education, health, sociability, economic productivity and reduced crime. These returns exceed the rate of return of stocks over the period of 1945–2008. Early childhood investments pay dividends for the life of the child. Each dollar invested returns 60–300 dollars over the lifetime. These programs pay out immediately and over the life of the child through a reduced burden on the schools in remediation, through a reduced burden on the criminal justice system and through enhanced college attendance and workforce productivity.

Invest money in quality programs. Comprehensive and cohesive early childhood education systems are desperately needed to reduce social disparities and their attendant economic costs. Quality early childhood education programs support parents to develop the package of cognitive and character skills necessary for learning, education achievement and college and career success. The programs also ensure that children receive needed health care and nutrition and assist parents in their role as their children's first and most important teacher. (Heckman, 2011)

MARIA MONTESSORI

With apologies to Erikson, Piaget, Vygotsky, and other eminent researchers and theorists of the past century who are not included here, Maria

Montessori demonstrated that solid early childhood learning theory could be put into practice.

Born in 1870 in Chiaravalle, Italy, Montessori was the first woman to graduate from the University of Rome La Sapienza Medical School and one of the first female doctors in Italy. She was appointed director of an institution for the care of the mentally retarded and was able to help several of her 8-year-old students take the national tests in reading and writing with above average results. In 1907, she was asked to start a school for children in a housing project in Rome, which she called Casa dei Bambini, or Children's House.

The most common implementation of Montessori instruction is for 2½-year-olds to 6-year-olds, and these are often called Children's Houses after Montessori's first school. Mixed-age groups allow older children to learn classroom routines and help new or younger children observe proper procedures. Montessori's concept of the absorbent mind applies primarily to this group. Her belief in the importance of self-discovery is embedded in her instructional design. Montessori devised educational materials to meet the needs of sensitive periods in development related to language acquisition, sensory development, motor skill development, and social behavior development. Montessori also developed programs for infants and toddlers, and elementary classrooms for children ages 6 to 12.

Montessori's work is based on the belief that with quality early education, children from all levels of affluence can become good learners with good character. Her prominent resistance to the ideas of Mussolini caused her to be exiled before World War II, and she lived in Spain, India, and the Netherlands. She died in the Netherlands in 1952.

REGGIO EMILIA

Amid the farm fields and hills southeast of Parma in northern Italy is the small town of Reggio Emilia. It is known as one of the finest examples of community connection and involvement with the learning lives of children. After World War II, the citizens of Reggio Emilia and surrounding villages wanted a system of education based on respect, responsibility, and community. With the leadership of Loris Malaguzzi, they collectively developed a philosophy of learning that is now recognized around the world (Cadwell, 2002; Lewin-Benham, 2008).

It is difficult to describe the Reggio approach to education because it is not a curriculum or a program. It is based on these principles:

- Children will have some control over their learning.
- Children will learn through the rich sensory experiences of movement, touch, listening, seeing, and hearing.
- Children will have a relationship with other children and with learning materials.
- Children will learn many ways of expressing themselves, including speech, writing, music and art.

In Reggio Emilia, parents are expected to be involved in the school and in the learning process at home. A strong school committee is involved in learning about curriculum and planning, and influences local government. Teachers benefit from extensive staff development and build a collaborative learning relationship with students. Intellectual curiosity is valued. The organization of physical space values beauty and collaboration. Long-term projects, constructivist learning, and expression through the arts are valued.

The community philosophy of learning manages to include the High-Scope emphasis on quality preschool, the family connection of the Abecedarian Project and PAT, the emotional conditions and constructivist approach to learning of Montessori, the cohesive preschool to early elementary connections of the Harlem Children's Zone, and a strong community commitment to schools and learning.

FINLAND

In the 1970s and 1980s, Finland went through a period of educational reform. Up to that point, the Finns had a fairly typical European educational system with a tracking system that divided students into vocational or academic tracks at age 10, with generally mediocre results on international assessments in math and science. Over the past decade, the country's education system has become one of the highest performing in the world according to the Programme for International Student Assessment. In 2009, Finland's students scored third in reading, sixth in math, and second in science out of 65 countries participating in the exam. The country has one of the narrowest gaps in achievement between its highest- and lowest-performing schools, and on average spends less per pupil than the United States (Sahlberg, 2011).

It is especially interesting to consider Finland's experience because more than 20 years ago, it made a choice to make major changes in its system to try to improve the learning outcomes of its children, and in doing so improve the economic outcomes of the nation. Notwithstanding the much smaller size of the country and the generally more homogenous population, certain aspects of the Finnish system are worthy of consideration.

The Finnish schools downplay the use of standardized testing, using it typically only twice in the educational life of a student, and expecting teachers to have a strong working knowledge of their students levels and needs. Compulsory schooling starts in first grade, and includes an emphasis on social skills, movement, art, music, and play. Broad curriculum objectives are established for each grade, but teachers are not given strict guidelines as to how to teach these skills and content. Teachers are expected to use formative assessment to know what students can do and plan instruction according to student readiness.

High-quality day care and nursery-kindergarten are considered critical for developing the language, motor, and social skills necessary to prepare young children for academic learning success, and Finland has offered free universal day care for children from age 8 months to 5 years since 1990, and a year of preschool/kindergarten at age 6 since 1996. Most families take advantage of these free services, but the municipality will also pay mothers a stipend to stay home and provide home day care for the first 3 years.

The Finnish 9-year system of compulsory schooling goes from age 7 to 16. At that point, students can decide if they want to go to the college-prep school to complete upper secondary school, or if they want to attend the vocational high schools, where they can start to learn a trade. Students can switch between the high school options, however, and choosing the vocational track does not preclude a student from getting into a university.

Teaching in Finland is considered a high status position, even though teachers make less in gross salary and pay more taxes than the typical American teacher. University education is funded by the government, but teacher training openings are highly sought. A 3-year graduate school experience is required and most teachers in Finland come from the top tier of undergraduate students. Great teachers are a key ingredient to any great school. Great teachers working within a well-designed education system are a recipe for success.

CHAPTER 11 STUDY QUESTIONS

1. Who are the pathfinders in your school or district?

2. What allowed pathfinders like Weikart and Ramey to construct quality research projects that were unique to their time?

3. What allowed pathfinders like Montessori, Slavin, Canada, and Winter to construct quality learning projects that were unique to their time?

4. Why would noneducators like Lawrence and Heckman dedicate such energy to improving early childhood learning opportunities and outcomes?

5. What similarities and differences do you see between the United States and Reggio Emilia or Finland?

6. What must occur before we can have deep conversations about quality learning systems in our country?

Love of Learning   12

After the holidays comes that long stretch of months between the first of the year and spring break. If you mostly experience frustration and anxiety in your work as an educator, this can be a dreadfully long part of the school year, a segment of time you endure and hope will eventually pass. For every member of the noncommittee, this was a period of joy. Successful teachers love to see learning in their classrooms and learning in their own lives.

Although before the holidays only Mrs. Rhodes and Mrs. Peterson were using the entire inventory of essential skills, by the time they returned to school the others decided they would as well. They were not satisfied with a literacy-only focus. It was more work, they all agreed, to look at the whole child, but nothing else made sense. Mrs. Wheeler, Mrs. Samulski, and Ms. Scott joined in the K–1 discussion with Mrs. Rhodes and Mrs. Peterson. Mrs. Samuels and Mrs. Jackson in second grade, Ms. Sanchez and Mr. Wheaton in third grade, along with Mrs. Whitney and Mrs. Stanley from the support team made up the Grades 2–3 discussion group. They continued to meet in Mrs. Peterson's room after school on Tuesdays and Thursdays, enjoyed hot drinks while chatting for a few minutes, then gathered by group and began sharing questions and successes about assessment, grouping, specific students, and instructional materials.

"She said I was becoming fanatically formative like the rest of you," reported Ms. Scott to her kindergarten and first-grade cohorts, describing a conversation earlier in the day with an upper-grade-level teacher.

"What did you say to her?" asked Mrs. Peterson.

Before the young teacher could respond, Mrs. Rhodes interjected. "Fanatically formative. I could like that description."

Mrs. Peterson shot her a look, then turned back to Ms. Scott.

"I told her that every day I wake up wanting to get to my classroom. And every day I get a little bit better at knowing what my students need." Ms. Scott went on. "She told me I've gone over to the dark side." The young first-grade teacher laughed.

Mrs. Rhodes was humming and making an entry on her notepad. At the top, in her perfect kindergarten printing, emerged the words FANATICALLY FORMATIVE. When she was done, she smiled at her friends.

The next day, Junie came up to Mrs. Peterson just before lunchtime. "Mrs. Peterson?"

"Yes, Junie."

"My mom said to ask you if we could borrow some books. Like, to keep for a while?" Junie's voice went up at the end of the sentence to emphasize the question.

"Your mom wants more books? I send one home with you every night," Mrs. Peterson said with a puzzled voice. At the beginning of the year, she had tried unsuccessfully to get Junie's mom to practice reading with Junie at home.

"It's because of that Saturday morning parenting program. My mom learned that she should help me practice reading but that she should also just read to us for fun at bedtime. Now she wants to read to me and my sister every night, but we don't have a lot of books. My sister is only 4. I told my mom you might have some good books that we'd both like to hear," explained Junie patiently.

When Mrs. Peterson pulled Junie close and hugged her, the little first grader understood that Mrs. Peterson would find her some books.

> The place to improve the world is first in one's own heart and head and hands, and then work outward from there.
>
> Robert M. Pirsig

For teachers who have taken the time to build good relationships, establish classroom routines, get to know their students, and teach them at their instructional readiness level, the winter months are filled with wonder. These teachers watch as students move into learning spurts during which skills develop right before their eyes. They watch as students discover the confidence to help plan their own learning, discover new interests, reach out to other students with empathy, and cheer on their friends when they struggle and when they succeed. For many students in these classrooms of success, these are the months during which they fall in love with learning. There is a calm, focused, positive learning energy in the room. You can feel it.

Early childhood educators have long noted an important truth: Children who fall in love with learning are more motivated, engaged, independent, and successful learners throughout their lives. Most young children are naturally hungry to learn. The desire to know and to understand is considered a basic need (Hawking, 1988; Maslow, 1954). Aldous Huxley (1930) observed that *"Children are remarkable for their intelligence and ardor, for their curiosity, their intolerance of shams, the clarity and ruthlessness of their vision."*

Children are more likely to use a skill if they feel competent, find joy in its use, and are given time to practice to a level of deep understanding or application (Jacobs & Crowley, 2007; Salomon & Globerson, 1987).

In a famous study, Anderson, Wilson, and Fielding (1988) considered the effect of reading skills on the choice to read outside of school. The choice to practice reading, they suggested, would influence the way reading skills develop as students move through school and perhaps influence learning success throughout life. Studying fifth-grade students, they found that children at the 90th percentile in reading, who both enjoy and are good at reading, will spend an average of 21 minutes a day in choice reading, that is, reading on their own, outside of school. This works out to 1.8 million words of choice reading per year. A child at the 10th percentile, lacking both skills and enjoyment of the reading process, will spend just 6 seconds a day in choice reading outside of school, which works out to just 8,000 words per year.

In his classic article "Catch Them Before They Fall," Joseph Torgesen (1998) points to the urgency of helping young students build successful patterns of reading in the early years of school. He describes the consequences associated with failure to acquire early word reading skills, including negative attitudes toward reading, reduced opportunities for vocabulary growth, reduced development of reading comprehension strategies, and less actual

> Simply put, we are more likely to use the skills that give us a sense of joy and success.

practice in reading than other children (Torgesen, 1998). "Schools must focus powerfully on preventing the emergence of early reading weaknesses—and the enormous reading practice deficits that result from prolonged reading failure—through excellent core classroom instruction and intensive, explicit interventions for children who are identified through reliable indicators as at risk of failure" (Torgesen, 2004). The best solution to the problem of reading failure is to prevent it! Children who are given the support to build early literacy skills and find success and joy while reading and writing become better readers and writers (Strickland & Walker, 2004).

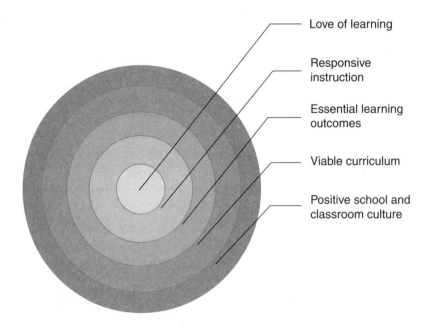

Love of learning

Responsive
instruction

Essential learning
outcomes

Viable curriculum

Positive school and
classroom culture

If we commit to helping students become engaged learners for life, we must:

- **Build a positive school and classroom culture**, which includes taking the time to build relationships, establish clear procedures, teach appropriate behavior, explore beauty and nature, model empathy and respect, develop schoolwide standards for behavior, develop a respectful adult community of learners, build the expectation of collaboration and ongoing teacher and parent learning, build trust, and present a positive emotional experience for learners, educators, and families.
- **Offer a viable curriculum to students**, which is a set of learning expectations that are manageable in the time available. This curriculum offers teachers the time to use excellent teaching techniques, reteach important content if needed, extend learning for those who are ready, help children learn essential content to a deep level of understanding and application, and allow time for play, language, nature, art, beauty, classroom culture building, reaching out to parents, and collaborating with other educators.
- **Identify essential learning outcomes**. A curriculum describes what you plan to teach. Essential learning outcomes are the skills and behaviors educators commit to helping every child learn. Even if a child comes to school with delays based on experience, gender, trauma, or other factors, teachers will adjust instruction,

materials, or time to help this child develop the foundation for ongoing learning success.

- **Offer responsive instruction** that is matched to the needs of children and delivered at the correct level of difficulty to maximize attention, motivation, engagement, and learning. Responsive instruction is matched to the needs of the whole child and does not focus only on skills that are measured by standardized state assessments. For young children, responsive instruction includes helping them learn self-regulation skills, including self-calming, delayed gratification, persistence, respect for authority, play skills, social skills, and how to choose and plan their own learning activities. Responsive instruction includes language skills, phonologic skills, movement skills, behavior skills, literacy, numeracy, and organization skills. Responsive instruction considers the individual interests and needs of children, encourages choice, inspires imagination, and builds a child's belief in himself as a learner and as a person.
- **Inspire the love of learning.** Any reading program, math program, curriculum or school improvement initiative that does not include helping students fall in love with learning is off target. Scripted, one-size-fits-all, drill-and-kill instruction sucks the learning lifeblood from children and adults. Great teachers will always aspire to the immeasurable joy that comes with the love of learning.

Soon, Mrs. Rhodes had decorated the panel above her classroom door with a multicolored sign. *FANATICALLY FORMATIVE, ask me!* No one ever did.

The newly named fanatically formative noncommittee began a process they called "data meetings." At one meeting each week, the whole group got together and focused on one grade, considering the data that showed which students were demonstrating proficiency and discussing which were developing or struggling. These meetings focused their awareness of the data and helped them keep the information up to date. It helped them hone their formative assessment skills and prepared them to offer responsive instruction.

> Keep me away from the wisdom which does not cry, the philosophy which does not laugh, and the greatness which does not bow before children.
>
> Khalil Gibran

By March, Tyrel had reached proficiency in each of the first-grade math skills, and Mrs. Peterson celebrated with him. From this time on, Tyrel could act as a helper to other math students, join in advanced math projects, or extend his learning to second-grade math skills. His behavior skills were developing nicely, and phonologic and motor skills were solid, but his oral language skills and literacy skills were not yet proficient. There is still time, Mrs. Peterson told herself.

During the winter months, Mrs. Peterson could feel the flow of learning all around her. Her children were happy. One day after school, she noticed Ms. Scott was late for a fanatically formative meeting and went to her classroom to check on her. It was a crisp, sunny afternoon, and the sunlight warmed the reading center. It was there, sleeping on her rocking chair in the reading center, that Mrs. Peterson saw her young colleague and friend. For more than a moment she just watched. A quiet classroom. The hum of the heaters. Sunlight on the shoulders of the young teacher.

Going to her, Mrs. Peterson touched her shoulder. "Are you OK?"

Ms. Scott startled, then saw Mrs. Peterson and sat up with a smile. She stretched in the rocking chair.

"I fell asleep," said the young first-grade teacher.

"Was it a hard day?" asked Mrs. Peterson.

For a moment, Ms. Scott hesitated, looking around her classroom. "No," she said with richness in her voice. "It was an absolutely wonderful day. It was the kind of day I want to have again. Hundreds of days like this. It was that kind of day."

CHAPTER 12 STUDY QUESTIONS

1. Who were the teachers who helped you fall in love with learning?

2. Were there learning situations in which you fell out of love with a subject of learning?

3. What are the implications of the Anderson, Wilson, and Fielding (1988) study?

4. How well do you help children fall into love with learning?

5. Do you have a support group to help you continue to develop your skills as a teacher or administrator?

Critical Thinking 13
Followed by Action

In every school, there are great educators restlessly waiting to make a positive change in the lives of students, build a working system far more successful than ours today, and ready to do the work of transformational change in their school and district. This chapter is for you. It is divided into sections for building or district administrators, classroom teachers, and parents. This is the how-to section, but it is not intended to be a scripted one-size-fits-all process. Consider this a model, which you will need to adapt to fit your specific needs and circumstances.

Meaningful change is a process. It probably won't happen as fast as you want. Building a vibrant early learning success initiative will take 3 to 5 years in most circumstances. It involves learning new skills and unlearning old patterns. In the process teachers will learn to use formative assessment as a part of instructional design, develop the discipline to keep formative assessment data up to date, design instruction based on this knowledge of students, work within a calm, safe, connected classroom environment, work within a consistent positive school culture, collaborate with grade-level colleagues and support team members, learn together, solve problems together, reach out to parents, and more. Central office administrators, principals, and parents all have important roles in this process. And hopefully it will be one of the most exciting learning adventures of your life.

BUILDING OR DISTRICT ADMINISTRATORS

1. *Begin the conversation.* Share articles and books about early learning success, formative assessment, collaboration, instructional match, responsive instruction.

> Dare mighty things.
> —Teddy Roosevelt

Find teacher-leaders who are willing to chair book clubs, professional learning communities (PLCs), and deeper conversations.

2. *Planning process.* Identify district/school leaders for a study and planning process. Assume that this will take several meetings and several months. Include strong leaders in the process, even if they are not yet supporters of a change initiative. The facts and research will bring them along.

- After a discussion of the purposes of the study group, use the Reflection on the Early Learning Success Initiative in Our School (Appendix J) to help you identify strengths and needs.
- Consider research questions. If there are points of research you need to explore, assign responsibility to gather the information and bring it back to the group.
- Identify the outcomes you want to accomplish in this 3-year to 5-year initiative. Choose outcomes that fit the specific needs of your school/district. For example,
  - We will identify and implement a system of universal screening and progress monitoring that defines essential K–3 outcomes.
  - A system of accountability will be fully implemented to ensure proper implementation of progress monitoring toward essential outcomes.
  - A system of instructional support will be designed and implemented, with clear procedures and time lines.
  - A culture of professional trust and collaboration will be explicitly defined and established.
  - A culture of respectful behavior management in the classroom and school will be established.
  - An active and respectful working relationship with parents will be planned and implemented.
  - An ongoing system of professional learning to support learning success for all students will be developed and implemented.
- Construct a specific measurable 3-year to 5-year plan with time lines and responsibilities noted for each of your outcomes (Sample District Plan for Early Learning Success in Appendix K).
- Pull together all the Year 1 steps and responsibilities and analyze this to see if you have a manageable plan for Year 1. There is a good chance you have put too much into your Year 1 plan. Set yourself up to succeed. Pare down the Year 1 plan if needed, and then revise all the other long-term outcome plans accordingly.
- Review your Year 1 plan. Look for any parts of the plan that are unclear or unmanageable. Once your Year 1 plan is clear, consider how it will be communicated to the school/district staff. Develop a

communication plan that includes pilot schools, pilot grades, pilot teachers, principals, central office staff, school board, parents, and other interested persons.

NOTES ON THE PLANNING PROCESS

Look to your better schools and teachers when planning to implement your early learning success initiative. A school with a significantly negative culture will not be an ideal pilot site. Find good leaders among principals and teachers when choosing implementation sites. A school with a positive culture is capable of much better learning and problem-solving than a negative school. A positive teacher leader makes a much better first-year implementer than a resistant teacher forced into the process.

Include use of an essential outcomes progress-monitoring process in the Year 1 classrooms, grade levels, or schools. Our experience is clear on this point. Significant changes in the use of formative assessment and responsive instruction in the classroom *do not occur* if you use the essential outcomes as an occasional or end-of-marking-period assessment. Proper use of the ongoing formative assessment process is necessary to change patterns of curriculum-driven instruction. Follow the Protocol for Use of the Essential Skills Inventories in K–3 (Appendix E).

Compassionate classroom/school culture and an effective support team are crucial to building an effective early learning initiative. If school culture is negative, this may need to be prioritized in the first year of your plan. If school culture is adequate, proceed to develop your essential skill progress-monitoring process, but come back to culture when possible. School culture must be respectful and empathetic for students or staff to learn at the highest levels. Developing a support team can happen in Year 1 or Year 2, depending on staff availability and your ability to devote time and energy for this purpose.

3. *Implementation.* You have taken on a long-term multifaceted change initiative. Create a support system to help you follow your plan to completion. If several schools in your district are working as pilot schools, schedule time for those principals and teacher leaders to meet and share challenges and successes. Schedule time for grade-level teachers within a school to meet and discuss assessment and instruction issues as they learn to offer responsive instruction. Teachers doing progress monitoring toward the essential outcomes should have monthly data meetings with the principal. Principals guiding Early Learning Success schools should have regular reviews with central office leaders to get ongoing support and to ensure that timelines are met. Plan to have an end-of-year meeting with key partners in the process to review your annual goals, progress, challenges, what you've learned, and to adjust plans/goals for the following year.

Common implementation challenges include the following:

- Teachers do not know how to use observational assessment to help determine proficiency. They have been trained to use standardized, textbook-provided, or district-provided paper-and-pencil assessments and may not be confident in their ability to observe proficient skills within classroom behavior and learning activities.

- Teachers are overwhelmed at the beginning of the year and do not know how to collect baseline essential outcome data.
- Teachers try to focus on designing instruction for essential outcomes but cannot let go of old patterns and are still trying to cover the overwhelming curriculum expectations, and so they try to do both.
- Teachers will need time to learn how to integrate available instructional material into whole-group lessons, small-group lessons, and instructional activities designed to help students build proficiency in the essential skills.
- Specific aspects of the essential outcomes are unfamiliar to the teacher (i.e., oral language, motor skills, visual memory, or delayed gratification). The teacher is afraid to ask for help because she is uncomfortable discussing her lack of experience with this aspect of development.
- Teachers tend to let essential skill data collection slide and go several weeks without updating their inventory.
- Principals get busy and are not available for regular data meetings with teachers.
- It is difficult to find time available for identified support team members to respond to requests for help.
- Support team procedures are unclear (Appendix L, Sample Support Team Procedures).
- Staff don't remember what you told them about making referrals to the support team and cannot identify how to begin the process.
- Support team members are used to problem solving but not very good at collaborating. Their tendency to make suggestions or offer to help is getting in the way of collaboration. Classroom teachers don't feel like the support team members are listening to them.
- Support team members fail to respond quickly to teacher requests.
- Some teachers do not have skills to manage student behavior without anger.
- Some teachers do not like to follow the school's written procedures for common spaces and allow their students to run in the halls, push others, speak disrespectfully to staff, or take cuts in line at lunch.
- Some teachers have poor social skills and do not realize they use intimidating behaviors with other staff members.
- A staff member does not typically practice the respectful behaviors with parents we have included in our plan to get more parents connected to the school.

The learning and problem-solving demands of this process are considerable. Available training and on-site coaching is an important support to teachers and principals. Contact the Early Learning Foundation (earlylearningfoundation.com) for information about training and coaching for your initiative.

4. *Evaluation.* Consider the things you want to measure as outcomes and as behaviors that support program integrity, and build these into your plan. You will probably want to measure how your initiative affects special education rates, since this is likely an economic benefit to your district. Measures of learning outcomes can be accomplished with tools you are already using in most cases. DRA, Standardized Test for the Assessment of Reading (STAR), and other measures of reading skills can show individual and classroom improvement patterns. The PreK–Grade 3 Essential Math Skills Inventory (Appendix N) is a progress monitoring tool that can be used as an ongoing assessment of math skills. Because your Essential Skills Inventory (ESI) is your richest source of data, you may find that you can reduce the number of standardized testing tools or district quarterly assessments because you already have formative data that meet your needs to monitory progress.

Your standardized state assessment is a poor tool for measuring outcomes but can be used to show positive growth in comparison to other districts. Measures of staff behaviors that support program integrity are more important than outcome measurements for building a learning culture focused on early learning success.

Outcomes measures during the years of your initiative can include the following:

- Number/rate of special education referrals
- Rate of special education referrals found eligible
- Referrals to your support team
- Percentage of students with special education labels in each school/district
- Rate of case closure for support team referrals per year
- Rates of satisfaction for classroom teachers making referrals to the support team
- DRA, STAR, and other measures of reading skill
- End of year rates of proficiency for essential grade level skills. The Essential Skills Inventory gives you formative data on all aspects of grade-level development but must be implemented with fidelity to get accurate information about student progress. A school/district could measure the percentage of students who achieve full proficiency in each segment of the inventory or on the entirety of grade-level outcomes.
- Student adherence to schoolwide procedures in the halls, the lunchroom, and on the playground
- Rates of student discipline referrals

- Parent surveys on school culture
- Teacher surveys on school culture

Measures of staff behaviors that support program integrity include the following:

- Rate of teachers who have established baseline ESI data by the end of 6 weeks
- Rate of teachers who update at least two segments of ESI data weekly
- Completion of monthly data meetings between principal and grade-level teachers
- Response by support team staff to referring teachers within 48 hours
- Adherence to support team procedures (Sample Support Team Procedures in Appendix L)
- Completion of quarterly school progress reviews with principal and designated central office administrator
- Teacher "good news" communications to parents per week/month
- Observational measures of staff greetings to students, staff, and parents

CLASSROOM TEACHERS

1. Classroom teachers committed to early learning success for every student should build a support network with other educators. Find a few like-minded individuals who can engage in the learning process with you and support each other along the way.

2. Read. Find sites of best practice. Become well-informed so that you are prepared to respond to the challenges to formative assessment and responsive instruction that will surely come your way.

3. Identify your goals for this school year. Try really hard not to take on too much. Pace yourself.

4. In your goals, include use of the essential skills progress-monitoring process. More than any one tool, this will keep you on track to using formative assessment and responsive instruction. Proper use of this process is necessary to change patterns of curriculum-driven instruction. Follow the Protocol for Use of the Essential Skills Inventories in K–3 (Appendix E). In your first year with this tool, you are unlikely to have all your students become proficient in each skill. If you help 75% of your students become proficient in every skill in your first year using the ESI, you will have been remarkably successful. Someday you will help more than 90% of your students become proficient in each of these skills.

5. When you encounter essential skills for your grade level that are not familiar subjects of instruction (oral language, delayed gratification, visual memory, organization skills, and phonologic skills are typical examples),

find help. Someone in your school is already an expert in this area. Don't reinvent the wheel. Instead, network!

6. When you encounter students who do not respond to typical instruction in your class, find help. Become good at asking others to help you accomplish your goals. Develop networks of learning with the best educators you know to help young students with delays catch up and succeed.

7. Help parents understand the importance of the development of proficient skills in these early years. Teach them about the effect of instructional match. Show them how much you know about their children from your skills inventory and promise them that this information helps you give them instruction at just the right level of difficulty to maximize learning. Your most engaged parents will become your allies in this process.

8. Include parents when you can. Reach out to parents and ask them to help their child develop a specific essential skill using the Building Essential Skills: Parent Support Request (Appendix O). Show them specifically how to help and make early learning fun.

PARENTS

1. You are your child's first teacher. As someone who is reading this book, we can assume that you are an unusually informed parent. Use the progression of skills in the Essential Skills Inventory, K–3 Outcomes (Appendix C) as a guide. Give your child learning experiences at home with a high rate of success to help him fall in love with learning. Make learning fun, especially in these crucial early learning years.

2. If your school is not engaged in an Early Learning Success Initiative, let's think first about your child. At the beginning of the kindergarten, first-grade, second-grade, and third-grade years, plan to build a relationship with your child's teacher. As soon as you have established a relationship with the teacher, it is time for an important conversation. Begin by sharing important information about your child.

Describe the following to the teacher:

- What's special about your child
- Her special interests
- Any special concerns you have for your child
- Your goals for this year

Then, ask a series of questions, which may be unfamiliar to this teacher, but which are important to help ensure that your child will have an optimal learning experience:

- What are the essential skills and behaviors she must learn this year to be ready for great success in subsequent years?
- How will you (the teacher) assess which of these skills she already has?
- Can you give her instruction at the correct level of challenge (instructional match)?
- Can you give her enough time to develop these skills to a deep level of understanding and application?
- Can you move her on to more advanced skills when she is ready?
- Can you prioritize helping her fall in love with learning?
- What can we (parents) do to help?

3. If your school is not engaged in an Early Learning Success Initiative, consider everyone's children. Share articles and books about early learning success, instructional match, formative assessment, responsive instruction, class culture, and school culture with the principal, and with any teachers you know and love. Be assertive without being adversarial. Find community support for developing a commitment to action supporting quality preK–Grade 3 programs.

4. Work with school leaders to develop a center for parent learning at your school. Ask to be involved in the development of a 5-year plan to help your school identify areas of interest for parent learning, resources for parent learning, and parent or teacher leaders who can offer ongoing training in many aspects of child development, including oral language development, literacy, numeracy, behavior skill development, movement skills and exercise, nutrition, and more. Emphasize the development of trusting relationships and professional respect throughout the development of a center for parent learning.

CHAPTER 13 STUDY QUESTIONS

1. Describe your first step toward developing a successful early learning success initiative.

2. After using the Reflection on the Early Learning Success Initiative in Our School (Appendix J), describe the strengths and weaknesses of your early learning success practices.

3. What books and articles should be in your school/district early learning success library?

4. How will you explain the importance of grade-level essential skills to parents?

5. Why are measures of staff behaviors that support program integrity more important than outcome measurements in building a successful initiative?

The Lives of Children in the Balance

14

"Mrs. Peterson?" It was a cool spring day. The sky was clear and a deep azure blue, and the children were on the playground. Tyrel had left his friends on the soccer field and come to stand next to his teacher. "Are you mad at me?"

"Tyrel, why would I be mad at you?" she asked with surprise.

"You just seem mad," he said softly. "Your voice seems mad when you talk to me lately."

The first-grade teacher bent down to his level and took both his hands. "No, Tyrel. I am not mad."

"Did I do something bad?"

"No. Why do you say that?"

"Sometimes when I'm in class, you look at me and your forehead gets all wrinkly, like you're upset," he explained.

She looked at Tyrel. He'd grown taller this year. His face was a little leaner. Some of the baby fat in his face was gone. Mrs. Peterson hugged him and sent him back to play.

For a while then, the world went quiet. Her students were playing in the bright sun, and one part of the first-grade teacher watched them out of habit, but her listening had moved elsewhere. She'd been worrying lately, stressing herself and apparently stressing her students. Mrs. Peterson wondered how often she'd furrowed her brow lately while working to keep her promise. She knew she'd been pressing. She'd justified it somehow. All these children will have the skills they need to succeed, she had promised herself. And almost all her students had achieved proficiency in every essential first-grade skill. Joel and Jason were still quirky, but their gross motor skills were good now and they'd learned to play well with others. Suzie

125

and Leroy were still strong-willed, but they'd turned into leaders. Jimmy, Abigail, and Kendra were still working on sight words and spelling with common words patterns, but they were close to proficient and would soon reach the standard. Even Junie. After the winter holiday, she had the most amazing burst of language learning. She was writing beautiful full paragraphs now, and greeting children and teachers in the hallway.

Only Tyrel and Jessica, her little cipher, would not reach proficiency on all the first grade essential skills. Jesse was still quiet in class, but she was happy now. She engaged in every learning activity but still had only three girls with whom she regularly talked. Sometimes Leroy could make her laugh. Jesse still could not skip. Her drawings lacked detail. She read words well, but usually her voice was mechanical and some days she could not describe what happened in the story. Tyrel had made so much progress. His phonologic skills, reading skills, motor skills, and math skills were solid. He was halfway through second-grade math outcomes. But some days it was so difficult for him to delay gratification, his vocabulary was still below level, and sustained listening was tough. And every day he tries so hard to learn, she thought.

At home that evening, she sat in the family room with her son. "I just haven't found a way to get it done," she said to him.

Matt nodded.

"It's not for lack of trying. I've never done more learning in my life than this year."

"We were watching. It was amazing how hard you worked."

"I thought for sure I could learn to be formative and responsive enough to keep my promise."

"I know what you mean," replied her big son.

"How can you know what that's like?"

"I came up short on one of my goals this year, too," Matt replied.

"What goal?"

"I promised I'd teach you to be technologically competent before I left for college. Not doing so well, are we?"

Mrs. Peterson smiled at her big son. In a few months he'd be off to college. "You tried. It's been a busy year, and I guess it's been easy to just let you do the more difficult tech tasks for me."

"I won't be as close by and available next year," said Matt.

"I can get your dad to help me. But you know how much faster you are than him," she said to her son.

"You can still learn any tech skills you need," Matt assured her. "Just because I won't be home much doesn't stop you from learning. You get good at it by doing it more. It just takes time."

She nodded. "That's sounds similar to my work at school this year. I thought I could learn to be expert at formative assessment and responsive instruction in 1 year, but now I realize I'm only beginning to develop my skills."

"So you need more time to really learn the skills to teach this way. What else do you need?" Matt asked.

"A good support group, plenty of patience, and an unwavering commitment. That's all," replied his mother.

As a nation, we have thus far failed to recognize the critical nature of early childhood learning. We have used old patterns of curriculum-driven instruction and rigid pacing systems to create anxious school environments in which both teachers and students are stressed and under-performing. In America 67% of our children are scoring below proficient reading levels at the beginning of fourth grade on the National Assessment of Educational Progress reading test (Annie Casey Foundation, 2010). Of these, 34% read at the *basic* level and 33% read at the *below basic* level. Among children living in poverty, 83% of fourth graders have reading skills below the proficient level (Hernandez, 2011) and three quarters of students who are poor readers in third grade will remain poor readers in high school (Shaywitz et al., 1997). We are on the path to allowing millions of our children to become damaged learners in the information age.

> Our goal as a nation must be to make sure that no child is denied the chance to grow in knowledge and character from the very first years.
>
> Fred Rogers

But this catastrophe can be averted. We can choose to develop quality early learning systems in which practically every child experiences early learning success. Consider the reasons for making this choice:

- First and foremost, early learning success affects the quality of life for each individual child. A lack of early learning success compromises the educational, economic, and social future of our children.
- Quality early learning systems save money for school districts by decreasing special education costs.
- Quality early learning systems improve academic outcomes, including graduation rates and test scores.
- Quality early learning systems improve social outcomes, including reduced at-risk behaviors, incarceration, and unemployment.
- Schools with positive classroom and school culture are better places for student learning and much better places for teachers to teach and collaborate.

- Positive school cultures are better able to build respectful learning relationships with parents.
- All our children need quality early learning systems. Helping children succeed and fall in love with learning during the early years is a necessary part of developing a nation of innovative and active learners.
- Poor children especially need quality early learning systems. To break the cycle of poverty, we must give children access to high-quality preschool and K–3 systems.
- Communities with quality early learning systems will produce more young men and women with self-regulation skills, academic skills, and social skills needed to be productive citizens and good neighbors.
- Nations with quality early learning systems will produce men and women more likely to be lifelong learners, innovators, collaborators, problem solvers, and caring citizens of the world.

HOW MAKE FIRE?

WORLD IS BROKEN. FIX IT.

RIGHT IDEA HARD. RIGHT IDEA HURT. RIGHT IDEA IS HOLE IN WORLD.

RIGHT IDEA MAKE BURN INSIDE TO FIX. CAN TAKE DAY OFF FROM IDEA? IT WRONG ONE.

FIND IDEA THAT BURN, GRAB WITH BOTH HANDS, NEVER LET GO.

THAT HOW MAKE FIRE.

Wilson (2011)

On the last day of school, there were some tears, and lots of laughter, and it was a happy day. School dismissed at lunchtime, and Tyrel's dad was waiting for him at the playground fence. Little presents and cards were left behind on her desk, but Mrs. Peterson left them unopened for now. She'd take them home and open them later.

A catered lunch was provided by the principal and the parent–teacher association, and afterwards the members of the fanatically formative noncommittee gathered in Mrs. Peterson's room. Each teacher had a room to organize, materials to put away, memories to store, emotions to process, but something had started this year and no one wanted it to end. They told stories and shared vacation plans. Principal Harris joined them. Still they lingered in conversation. Finally, Mrs. Rhodes called them to attention.

"It's been an extraordinary year, but I failed to meet my goal. Four of my students did not make proficiency in all the kindergarten goals. And I'm a darned good teacher." She looked powerfully around the room. "We all know how important it is to do this work, and yet it seems we have a lot to learn. Is this something we can learn to do well?"

"Those four students were so needy coming into kindergarten. How could you possibly catch them up?" said Ms. Sanchez.

"I don't yet know," replied the experienced kindergarten teacher.

The young first-grade teacher, Ms. Scott, spoke up. "I want some of those students. There is still plenty of time to help them become good learners." She glanced at Mrs. Peterson, who smiled back at her.

"We have to keep in mind that there will always be some children who aren't fully proficient by the end of a school year," added Mrs. Wheeler.

"But fewer and fewer each year, if we learn to do this well," said Mrs. Jackson.

"For me, there is a lot of learning ahead," offered Mr. Wheaton. "It's going to take a long-term commitment."

"This is something worth doing well," said Ms. Harris. "And we can do a lot more to build collaboration throughout the school and expand the role of the instructional support team."

"How do we make formative assessment and responsive instruction part of our school culture? To be successful, we will have to make it an expected part of good teaching around here," added Mrs. Samulski.

"And we can't forget the parents," said Mrs. Whitney. "We need their support and involvement."

"And someday we need a community commitment to early learning success," reminded Mrs. Stanley.

"I have to get better at being disciplined enough to update my inventory every week," said Ms. Scott. "I need to maintain an up-to-date data map to help me plan instruction."

Looking at her longtime friend, Mrs. Samuels said, "Mrs. Peterson, you dragged me into this formative assessment and responsive instruction thing. What's next?"

"At the beginning of the year, it scared me to think about changing the way I plan and deliver instruction, but I made a promise to my students," said Mrs. Peterson in reply. "Someday I hope we can put all the pieces in place within our school, but this work starts in our classrooms. I think we'll get much better at teaching responsively by doing it more. And with a support group like we've started this year, and plenty of patience, and an unwavering commitment, we can do this."

Each of the teachers had already considered a personal learning plan for the summer. Some were planning to attend a Prevention of Early Learning Failure Conference. A couple had book lists. The second-grade and third-grade teachers were working on aligning activities and lessons to their essential math skills. The kindergarten teachers were working on a behavioral skills curriculum. The group adjourned. Some hurried home to children. Some stayed at school into the early evening, organizing and cleaning their classrooms. Most would be back on the weekend, cleaning up, writing notes to children, filing information and reports. Throughout the summer, they met in small groups, sometimes found each other working in their classrooms, met for coffee, or shared dinner with each other's families.

Mrs. Peterson heard from many of her students during the summer. When she learned that Leroy was moving out of town, she invited all the class to meet at an ice cream shop for a going-away party. Twenty of the kids and their families were able to attend, but Tyrel wasn't there. She worried. A few days later, Tyrel's dad called and explained they'd been out of town. Yes, Tyrel would be back to school. Yes, they were reading the books she'd given them. Yes, they were having a great summer. And yes, they could come over to dinner next week.

CHAPTER 14 STUDY QUESTIONS

1. The teachers in this book have begun a mighty journey. How long will it take before they develop a sustainable schoolwide model of early learning success?

2. If your school decides to develop an early learning success initiative, what are reasonable goals for the first year?

3. Which of the characters in this book remind you of yourself? Why?

4. Are the educators in your school community ready to embrace the professional learning and collaboration needed for a successful early learning initiative?

5. What is your greatest motivation for wanting to be part of an early learning success initiative?

Appendixes

A. MRS. PETERSON'S FIRST-GRADE ESSENTIAL SKILLS INVENTORY: CLASS BASELINE DATA

Teacher: Mrs. Peterson — Baseline Data

Indicate mastery by writing mastery date to the right of the student's name and under the feature mastered

Area of Assessment	Letters		Phonologic Skills				Language			Motor Skills			Visualization			
	1	2	3	4	5	6	7	8	9	10	11	12	13	14	15	16
Essential Skills	Identifies uppercase letters	Identifies lowercase letters	Identifies a letter sound associated with each letter	Produces rhymes for a given word	Identifies beginning, middle, and ending sounds of words	Combines phonemes to make words	Uses age-appropriate vocabulary in speech	Uses language to solve problems	Demonstrates effective listening skills	Demonstrates appropriate balance	Demonstrates appropriate skipping	Uses comfortable near-point vision	Draws pictures with detail	Can tell or retell a story	Recognizes basic sight words	Follows print when reading (visual tracking)
Student Name																
Phillip	9–28	9–28	10–3	10–20	10–26	10–26	10–1	10–25		10–1	10–1	10–1		10–15		10–18
Jimmy	9–28	10–8	10–15	10–15				10–14	10–14					10–20		
Sarah	9–28	9–28	10–3	10–20	10–26	10–26	10–1	10–2	10–2	10–1	10–1	10–1	10–18	10–15		10–18
Abigail	10–15	10–30		10–15				10–14	10–14							
Kendra	10–15	10–15	10–15						10–18		10–1	10–1		10–18		10–18
Danny	9–28	9–28			10–26				10–14					10–18		
Junie	10–30															
Justin	9–28	9–28														
Tyrel	10–30	10–30														
Peter	9–28	9–28								10–18						10–18
Cassandra	9–28	9–28							10–14	10–18				10–18		10–18
Jessica	10–7	10–23	10–23											10–20		10–18
Suzie	9–28	9–28	10–15		10–26					10–1		10–1	10–16			10–18
Ralph	9–28	9–28	10–15		10–26					10–1		10–1				10–18
Joel	9–28	9–28	10–15									10–1				
Jason	9–28	9–28	10–15													
Justin	9–28	9–28	10–15	10–15	10–26					10–1	10–1			10–16		10–18
Samantha	9–28	9–28	10–3	10–15	10–26					10–1	10–1			10–16		10–18
Andrew	9–28	9–28	10–15													
Marcus	9–28	9–28	10–15													
Dylan	9–28	9–28	10–15									10–1				
Camilla	9–28	9–28	10–3	10–15	10–26				10–14	10–1	10–1	10–1	10–16			10–18
Katie	9–28	9–28	10–3	10–15	10–26				10–14	10–1	10–1	10–1	10–16			10–18

Literacy							Numeracy						Behavior		
17	18	19	20	21	22	23	24	25	26	27	28	29	30	31	32
Decodes grade-appropriate print	Reads short sentences	Reads for meaning	Prints 30 to 50 personally meaningful words	Expresses ideas in writing (simple sentences)	Spells using common word patterns	Spells words using visual memory	Counts objects with accuracy to 100	Replicates visual patterns or movement patterns	Recognizes number groups without counting (2 to 10)	Understands concepts of add on or take away (to 30) with manipulatives	Adds/subtracts single digit problems on paper	Shows a group of objects by number (to 100)	Delays gratification when necessary	Plays well with others	Shows interest in learning
10–4	10–18		10–4	10–4	10–18		10–22	10–19	9–25		10–6		10–15		10–1
									10–14				10–8	10–5	10–1
10–4	10–18		10–4	10–4	10–18		10–25	10–19	9–14		10–6		10–1	10–5	10–1
									10–14				10–8	10–5	10–5
							10–26						10–15		
							10–26						10–15		
							10–26								
10–25							10–25	10–19	9–14				10–15		
10–25							10–22	10–19	9–25				10–15	10–15	
10–18			10–8	10–8	10–18		10–22	10–19	9–25						
							10–22	10–19	10–14						
							10–22		9–25						10–5
							10–22		9–25						
10–4	10–18		10–8	10–8	10–18		10–22	10–19	9–25		10–6		10–1		10–5
							10–22	10–19	10–14				10–1		
							10–22	10–19	10–14						
							10–22	10–19	10–14				10–1	10–5	
	10–18		10–8	10–18			10–22	10–19	10–14		10–6		10–1	10–5	10–5
	10–18		10–8	10–18			10–22	10–19	10–14		10–6		10–1	10–5	10–5

B. REFERENCES FOR CONSIDERING ESSENTIAL EARLY LEARNING OUTCOMES

Literacy

Allington, R. (2005). *What really matters for struggling readers.* Boston, MA: Allyn & Bacon.

Allington, R. (2008). *What really matters in response to intervention.* Boston, MA: Allyn & Bacon.

Allington, R. L. (2001). *What really matters for struggling readers: Designing research-based programs.* New York, NY: Longman.

Boyer, E. (1995). *The basic school: A community for learning.* Stanford, CA: The Carnegie Foundation for the Advancement of Teaching.

Clay, M. (1985). *The early detection of reading difficulties* (3rd ed.). Portsmouth, NH: Heinemann Educational Books.

Clay, M. (1993). *An observation survey of early literacy achievement.* Portsmouth, NH: Heinemann Educational Books.

Clay, M. (2000). *Becoming literate: The construction of inner control.* Portsmouth, NH: Heinemann Educational Books.

Jensen, E. (2005). *Teaching with the brain in mind.* Alexandria, VA: ASCD.

Marzano, R. J. (1992). *A different kind of classroom: Teaching with dimensions of learning.* Alexandria, VA: ASCD.

Marzano, R. J. (2003). *What works in schools: Translating research into action.* Alexandria, VA: ASCD.

Marzano, R., Waters, T., & McNulty, B.A. (2005). *School leadership that works: From research to results.* Alexandria, VA Association for Supervision and Curriculum Development; Aurora, CO: Midcontinent Research for Education and Learning.

Marzano, R. J. (2007). *The art and science of teaching.* Alexandria, VA: ASCD.

Marzano, R. J., Pickering, D., & Pollock, J. E. (2001).*Classroom instruction that works: Research-based strategies for increasing student achievement.* Alexandria, VA: ASCD.

Snow, C. E., Burns, M. S., & Griffin, P. (Eds.). (1998). *Preventing reading difficulties in young children.* Washington, DC: National Academy Press.

Snow, C., Griffin, P., & Burns, M.S. (2005). *Knowledge to support the teaching of reading: preparing teachers for a changing world.* San Francisco, CA: Jossey-Bass.

Stanovich, K. (1994). Constructivism in reading education. *Journal of Special Education 28*(3), 259–274.

Torgesen, J. (1998). Catch them before they fall: Identification and assessment to prevent reading failure in young children. *American Educator, 22*(1–2), 32–39.

Torgesen, J., Rashotte, C. A., & Greenstein, J. (1988). Language comprehension in learning disabled children who perform poorly on memory span tests. *Journal of Educational Psychology, 80*(4), 480–487.

Vellutino, F. R. (1981). *Dyslexia theory and research.* Cambridge, MA: The MIT Press Classics Series.

Vellutino, F. R., Scanlon, D. M., & Tanzman, M. S. (1998). The case for early intervention in diagnosing specific reading disability. *Journal of School Psychology, 36,* 367–397.

Vellutino, F. R., Scanlon, D. M., Sipay, E. R., Small, S. G., Pratt, A., Chen, R., & Denckla, M. B. (1996). Cognitive profiles of difficult-to-remediate and readily remediated poor readers: Early intervention as a vehicle for distinguishing between cognitive and experiential deficits as basic causes of specific reading disability. *Journal of Educational Psychology, 88*(4), 601–638.

Instructional Match

Burns, M. K. (2007). Reading at the instructional level with children identified as learning disabled: Potential implications for response to intervention. *School Psychology Quarterly, 22,* 297–313.

Fuchs, D., & Fuchs, L.S. (2007).Increasing strategic reading comprehension with peer-assisted learning strategies. In D. S. McNamara (Ed.), *Reading comprehension strategies: Theories, interventions, and technologies* (pp. 175–197). Mahwah, NJ: Erlbaum.

Fuchs, L., & Fuchs, D. (1988).Curriculum-based measurement. A methodology for evaluating and improving student programs. *Assessment for Effective Intervention, 14*(1), 3–13.

Fuchs, L., Fuchs, D., & Hamlett, C. (1990). Curriculum-based measurement. A standardized, long-term goal approach to monitoring student progress. *Intervention in School and Clinic, 25*(5), 615–631.

Fuchs, L., Fuchs, D., Bishop, N., & Hamlett, C. (1992). Classwide decision-making strategies with curriculum-based measurement. *Assessment for Effective Intervention, 18*(1), 39–52.

Fuchs, L. S., & Fuchs, D. (2007)."Instruction on mathematical problem solving." In D. Berch & M. Mazzacco (Eds.), *Why is math so hard for some children? The nature and origins of mathematical learning difficulties and disabilities* (pp. 397–414). Baltimore, MD: Brookes.

Gickling, E. E., & Armstrong, D. L. (1978). Levels of instructional difficulty as related to on-task behavior, task completion, and comprehension. *Journal of Learning Disabilities, 11,* 32–39.

Gickling, E. E., & Havertape, S. (1981). *Curriculum-based assessment (CBA).* Minneapolis, MN: School Psychology Inservice Training Network.

Gickling, E. E., & Thompson, V. P. (1985). A personal view of curriculum-based assessment. *Exceptional Children, 52*(3), 205–218.

Kovaleski, J. (2007). Response to intervention: Considerations for research and systems change. *School Psychology Review, 36*(4), 638–646.

Kovaleski, J., Tucker, J. A., & Stevens, L. J. (1996). Bridging special and regular education: The Pennsylvania initiative. *Educational Leadership, 53*(5), 44–47.

Kovaleski, J., Tucker, J., Duffy, D., Lowery, P., & Gickling, E. (1995). School reform through instructional support: The Pennsylvania initiative. part I: The instructional support team (IST) part II: Instructional evaluation. *Communique, 23*(8), 24.

Rosenfield, S., & Gravois, T.A. (1996). *Instructional consultation teams: Collaborating for change.* New York, NY: Guilford Press.

Tucker, J. A. (2001), Instructional support teams: It's a group thing. B. Sornson (Ed.), *Preventing early learning failure.* Alexandria, VA: ASCD.

Vygotsky, L. S. (1978). *Mind in society: The development of higher psychological processes.* Cambridge, MA: Harvard University Press.

Phonologic Skills

Gillon, G. (2004). *Phonological awareness: From research to practice.* New York, NY: Guilford Press.

Kaminski, R. A., & Cummings, K. D. (2007). Assessment for learning: Using general outcomes measures. *Threshold, Winter, 26–28.*

Snow, C. E., Burns, M. S., & Griffin, P. (Eds.). (1998). *Preventing reading difficulties in young children.* Washington, DC: National Academy Press.

Speece, D., & Cooper, D. (1990). Ontogeny of school failure: Classification of first-grade children. *American Educational Research Journal, 27*(1), 119–140.

Speece, D., Mills, C., Ritchey, K., & Hillman, E. (2003). Initial evidence that letter fluency tasks are valid indicators of early reading skill. *Journal of Special Education, 36*(4), 223–233.

Speece, D., Ritchey, K., Cooper, D., Roth, F., & Schatschneider, C. (2004). Growth in early reading skills from kindergarten to third grade. *Contemporary Educational Psychology, 29*(3), 312–332.

Torgesen, J., Wagner, R., & Rashotte, C. (1994). Longitudinal studies of phonological processing and reading. *Journal of Learning Disabilities, 27,* 276–286.

Wagner, R. K., & Torgesen, J, K. (1987). The nature of phonological processing and its causal role in the acquisition of reading skills. *Psychological Bulletin,* 101, 192–212.

Walley, A. C., Metsala, J. L., & Garlock, V. M. (2003). Spoken vocabulary growth: Its role in the development of phoneme awareness and early reading ability. *Reading and Writing: An Interdisciplinary Journal, 16,* 5–20.

Oral Language

Chomsky, C. (1970). Reading, writing, and phonology. *Harvard Education, 40*(2) 287–309.

Chomsky, C. (1971). Write first, read later. *Childhood Education, 47*(6), 296–299.

Chomsky, C. (1976). After decoding: What? *Language Arts, 53*(3) 288–296, 314.

Clay, M. M., Gill, M., Glynn, T., McNaughton, T., & Salmon, K. (2007). *Record of oral language: Observing changes in the acquisition of language structures* (3rd ed.). New Zealand: Heinemann.

Dickinson, D. K., &. Tabors, P. O. (2002). Fostering language and literacy in classrooms and homes. *Young Children, 57,* 10–18.

Hart, B., & Risley, T. (2003).The early catastrophe. *The American Educator.* American Federation of Teachers. Retrieved from http://www.aft.org/newspubs/periodicals/ae/spring2003/hart.cfm

Healy, J. (1999). *Endangered minds: Why children don't think and what we can do about it.* New York, NY: Touchstone Books.

Levine, M. (2002). *A mind at a time.* New York, NY: Simon & Schuster.

Nation, K., & Snowling, M. J. (2004). Beyond phonological skills: Broader language skills contribute to the development of reading. *Journal of Research in Reading, 27,* 342–356.

Risley, T. R., & Hart, B. (1995). *Meaningful differences in the everyday experience of young American children.* Baltimore, MD: Brookes.

Shaywitz, S. E., & Shaywitz, B. A. (2004). The new science of reading and its implications for the classroom. *Education Canada, 44*(1), 20–23.

Snow, C. E., & Sweet Polselli, A. P. (2003). Reading for comprehension. In A. Polselli Sweet & C. E. Snow (Eds.), *Rethinking reading comprehension* (pp. 1–11). New York, NY: Guilford Press.

Stanovich, K. E., & Stanovich, P. J. (1995). How research might inform the debate about early reading acquisition. *Journal of Research in Reading, 18*(2), 87–105.

Gross Motor Skills

Dennison, P., & Dennison, G. (1986). *Brain gym. Simple activities for whole brain learning.* Glendale, CA: Edu-Kinesthetics.

Hannaford, C. (2005). *Smart moves: Why learning is not all in your head.* Salt Lake City, UT: Great River Books.

Jensen, E. (2005). *Teaching with the brain in mind.* Alexandria, VA: ASCD.

Liddle, T. L., & Yorke L. (2003). *Why motor skills matter.* New York, NY: McGraw-Hill.

Piaget, J. (1952). *The origins of intelligence in children.* New York, NY: International University Press.

Pica, R. (2004). *Experiences in movement: Birth to age eight.* Clifton Park, NY: Delmar Learning.

Ratey, J. (2008). *Spark: The revolutionary new science of exercise and the brain.* New York, NY: Little, Brown.

Sornson, N. (2012). *Motor skills for academic success.* Brighton, MI: Early Learning Foundation.

Sylwester, R. (1995). *A celebration of neurons: An educator's guide to the human brain.* Alexandria, VA: ASCD.

Visual Motor Skills

Ayers, A. (1972). Improving academic scores through sensory integration. *Journal of Learning Disabilities, 5*(6), 338–343,

Hannaford, C. (2005). *Smart move: Why learning is not all in your head.* Salt Lake City, UT: Great River Books.

Kranowitz, C. (2005). *The out-of-sync child: Recognizing and coping with sensory processing disorder.* London, England: Perigee Press.

Miller, L. (1984). Sources of visual field interference in children and adults. *Journal of Experimental Child Psychology, 37*(1), 141–157.

Rayner, K. (1978). Eye movements in reading and information processing. *Psychological Bulletin, 85*(3), 618–660.

Rayner, K. (1986). Eye movements and the perceptual span in beginning and skilled readers. *Journal of Experimental Child Psychology, 41*(2), 211–236.

Rayner, K. (1997). Understanding eye movements in reading. *Scientific Studies of Reading, 1*(4), 317–339.

Rourke, B. P. (1989). *Nonverbal learning disabilities: The syndrome and the model.* New York, NY: Guilford Press.

Rourke, B. P. (Ed.). (1991). *Neuropsychological validation of learning disability subtypes.* New York, NY: Guilford Press.

Rourke, B. P. (Ed.). (1995). *Syndrome of nonverbal learning disabilities: Neurodevelopmental manifestations.* New York, NY: Guilford Press.

Schneider, C. (2006). *Sensory secrets.* Northville, MI: The Concerned Group.

Sornson, N. (2012). *Motor skills for academic success.* Brighton, MI: Early Learning Foundation.

Numeracy

Anghileri, J. (1989). An investigation of young children's understanding of multiplication. *Educational Studies in Mathematics, 20*(4), 367–385.

Anghileri, J. (2006). Scaffolding practices that enhance mathematics learning. *Journal of Mathematics Teacher Education, 9*(1), 33–52.

Bobis, J. (2008). Early spatial thinking and the development of number sense. *Australian Primary Mathematics Classroom, 13*(3), 4–9.

Thomas, G., Tagg, A., & Ward, J. (2002). Making a difference: The Early Numeracy Project. In Barton, B., Irwin, K., Pfannkuch, M., & Thomas, M. (Eds.) (2002). *Mathematics education in the South Pacific.* Proceedings of the 25th annual conference of the Mathematics Education Resarch Group of Australasia (pp. 49–57). Sydney, Australia: MERGA.

Behavioral and Social Skills

Adler, A. (1956). *The individual psychology of Alfred Adler* (H. L. Ansbacher & R. R. Ansbacher, Eds.). New York, NY: Harper Torchbooks.

Bondy, E., & Ross, D. D. (2008). The teacher as warm demander. *Educational Leadership, 66*(1), 54–58.

Bondy, E., Ross, D. D., Gallingane, C., & Hambacher, E. (2007). Creating environments of success and resilience. Culturally responsive classroom management and more. *Urban Education, 42*(4), 326–348.

Cline, F. W., & Fay, J. (2006). *Parenting teens with love and logic.* Golden, CO: Love and Logic Press.

Cline, F. W., & Fay, J. (1990). *Parenting with love and logic: Teaching children responsibility.* Colorado Springs, CO: Pinon Press.

Coloroso, B. (1995). *The bullies, the bullied, and the bystanders.* New York, NY: Harper Collins.

Coloroso, B. (2005). *Kids are worth it.* New York, NY: Harper Collins.

Coloroso, B. (2011). Bully, bullied, bystander . . . and beyond. *Teaching Tolerance, 39,* 50–53.

Fay, J., Cline, F. W., & Sornson, B. (2000). *Meeting the challenge.* Golden, CO: Love and Logic Press.

Glasser, W. (1969). Schools without failure. *Instruction, 78*(5), 60–61.

Glasser, W. (1998). *Choice theory: A new psychology of personal freedom.* New York, NY: Harper Collins.

Goleman, D. (1995). *Emotional intelligence: Why it can matter more than IQ.* New York, NY: Bantam.

Goleman, D. (1996). Emotional intelligence. Why it can matter more than IQ. *Learning, 24*(6), 49–50.

Horner, R. H., Sugai, G., & Horner, H. F. (2000). A schoolwide approach to student discipline. *School Administrator, 57*(2), 20–23.

Mendler, A. (1992). *What do I do when . . . ? How to achieve discipline with dignity in the classroom.* Bloomington, IN: Solution Tree.

Mendler, A. (2000). *Motivating students who don't care: Successful techniques for educators.* Bloomington, IN: National Educational Service.

Sugai, G., & Horner, R. H. (2008). What we know and need to know about preventing problem behavior in schools. *Exceptionality, 16*(2), 67–77.

The Whole Child

Brazelton, T. B., & Greenspan, S. I. (2007). Why children need experiences tailored to their uniqueness. *Early Childhood Today, 3*(21), 10–11.

Brazelton, T. (1995). Readiness begins at birth. *Principal, 74*(5), 6–7, 9.

Brazelton, T., & Greenspan, S. (2000). *The irreducible needs of children: What every child must have to grow, learn, and flourish.* New York, NY: Perseus Publishing.

Brazelton, T., & Greenspan, S. I. (2006). The need for developmentally appropriate experiences. *Early Childhood Today, 3*(21), 16–17.

Caine, R. N., & Caine, G. (1991). *Making connections: Teaching and the human brain.* Wheaton, MD: ASCD.

Comer, J. P. (1989). *Maggie's American dream: The life and times of a black family.* New York, NY: Penguin Group.

Elias, S. F., & Elias, J. W. (1976). Curiosity and openmindedness in open and traditional classrooms. *Psychology in the Schools, 13*(2), 226–232.

Erikson, E. H. (1959). Identity and the life cycle. New York, NY: International Universities Press.

Erikson, E. H. (1968). *Identity, youth and crisis.* New York, NY: Norton.

Greenspan, S. I., DeGangi, G., & Wieder, S. (2001). *The functional emotional assessment scale (FEAS): For infancy & early childhood.* Bethesda, MD: Interdisciplinary Council on Development & Learning Disorders.

Greenspan, S. I., & Lewis, N. B. (1999). *Building healthy minds: The six experiences that create intelligence and emotional growth in babies and young children.* Cambridge, MA: Perseus Publishing.

Greenspan, S. I., & Greenspan, N. T. (1985). *First feelings: Milestones in the emotional development of your baby and child.* New York, NY: Viking.

Gregorc, A. (1984). Style as a symptom: A phenomenological perspective. *Theory Into Practice, 23*(1), 51–55.

Kagan, S. (1990). The structural approach to cooperative learning. *Educational Leadership, 47*(4), 12–15.

Kagan, S. (2001).Teaching for character and community. *Educational Leadership, 59*(2), 50–55.

Kaminski, R. A. (1992). *Assessment for the primary prevention of early academic problems: Utility of curriculum-based measurement prereading tasks.* University of Oregon, Eugene, OR.

Kline, P. (1988). *The everyday genius.* Marshall, NC: Great Ocean Publishers.

Montessori, M. (1967). *The absorbent mind.* New York, NY: Delta.

Montessori, M. (1995). Education in relation to the imagination of the little child. *NAMTA Journal, 20*(3), 42–49.

Montessori, M., & Montessori, M. (1995). Peace through education. *NAMTA Journal, 20*(3), 53–58.

Piaget, J. (1932). *The moral judgment of the child.* London, England: Kegan Paul, Trench, Trubner and Co.

Piaget, J. (1952). *The origins of intelligence in children.* New York, NY: International University Press.

Piaget, J. (1972). Intellectual evolution from adolescence to adulthood. *Human Development, 15*(1), 1–12.

Sornson, B. (2012). *Essential skills inventories K–3.* Brighton, MI: Early Learning Foundation.

Sylwester, R. (1994). How emotions affect learning. *Educational Leadership, 52*(2), 60–65.

Sylwester, R. (1995). *A celebration of neurons: an educator's guide to the human brain.* Alexandria, VA: ASCD.

Sylwester, R. (2005). *How to explain a brain: An educator's handbook of brain terms and cognitive processes.* Thousand Oaks, CA: Corwin.

Sylwester, R. (2007). *The adolescent brain: Reaching for autonomy.* Thousand Oaks, CA: Corwin.

Weikart, D. P., & Schweinhart, L. J. (1991). Disadvantaged children and curriculum effects. *New Directions for Child Development, 53*, 57–64.

Weikart, D., Bond, J. T., & McNeil, J. T. (1978). *The Ypsilanti Perry Preschool Project.* Ypsilanti, MI: HighScope.

C. ESSENTIAL SKILLS INVENTORY, K–3 OUTCOMES

Kindergarten Essential Skills Inventory

Shapes
- Identifies basic shapes
- Draws basic shapes

Visual
- Uses hands and eyes at near point
- Maintains visual focus at near point

Letters
- Identifies uppercase letters
- Identifies lowercase letters

Phonologic Skills
- Identifies if sounds are the same or different
- Identifies rhyming words
- Produces rhymes for a given word
- Identifies beginning or ending sounds of words
- Blends given sounds into words
- Segments words into sounds
- Listens with interest to stories
- Identifies a letter sound associated with each letter

Language
- Asks questions when appropriate
- Follows two-part oral directions
- Uses age-appropriate vocabulary
- Uses language to solve problems

Motor Skills
- Demonstrates throwing and catching skills with a small ball
- Can balance on one foot with eyes closed for 6 seconds
- Skips well for at least 10 yards

Literacy
- Understands concepts of print
- Recognizes personally meaningful sight words
- Prints 10 to 20 personally meaningful words
- Uses letter-sound knowledge to write words
- Prints full name

Numeracy
- Demonstrates counting to 100
- Has one-to-one correspondence for numbers 1 to 30
- Understands combinations (to 10)
- Recognizes number groups without counting (2–10)

Behavior
- Perseveres to achieve a task
- Respects basic rules/procedures in the classroom

First-Grade Essential Skills Inventory

Letters

- Identifies uppercase letters
- Identifies lowercase letters

Phonologic Skills

- Identifies a letter sound associated with each letter
- Produces rhymes for a given word
- Identifies beginning, middle, and ending sounds of words
- Combines phonemes to make words

Language

- Uses age-appropriate vocabulary in speech
- Uses language to solve problems
- Demonstrates effective listening skills

Motor Skills

- Demonstrates appropriate balance
- Demonstrates appropriate skipping
- Uses comfortable near-point vision

Visualization

- Draws pictures with detail
- Can tell/retell a story

Literacy

- Recognizes basic sight words
- Follows print when reading (visual tracking)
- Decodes grade-appropriate print
- Reads short sentences
- Reads for meaning
- Prints 30 to 50 personally meaningful words
- Expresses ideas in writing (simple sentences)
- Spells using common word patterns
- Spells words using visual memory

Numeracy

- Counts objects with accuracy to 100
- Replicates visual patterns or movement patterns
- Recognizes number groups without counting (2–10)
- Understands concepts of add on or take away (to 30) with manipulatives
- Can add or subtract single digit problems on paper
- Shows a group of objects by number (to 100)

Behavior

- Delays gratification when necessary
- Plays well with others
- Shows interest in learning

© Early Learning Foundation

Second-Grade Essential Skills Inventory

Reading

- Uses phonics knowledge to decode words in context
- Recognizes basic sight words
- Reads with fluency
- Reads for pleasure
- Identifies story elements
- Identifies main ideas
- Makes text-to-text connections
- Makes text-to-self connections
- Makes inferences when reading

Visual Memory

- Spells using visual memory
- Can remember three-block visual patterns

Language

- Uses age-appropriate vocabulary
- Demonstrates effective listening skills
- Uses language to recognize feelings in self and others

Writing

- Prints neatly
- Writes in full sentences
- Spells using phonics skills
- Makes simple revisions to a draft
- Writes using rich detail

Motor Skills

- Demonstrates excellent balance and skipping

Mathematics

- Quickly recognizes number groups (to 100)
- Can show a group of objects by number (to 100)
- Can add on or take away from a group of objects (to 100)
- Can add or subtract double-digit problems on paper
- Counts by 2, 3, 4, 5, and 10 using manipulatives
- Solves written and oral story problems using the correct operations
- Understands/identifies place value to 1,000

Behavior

- Demonstrates empathy for fellow students
- Shows interest in learning

Third-Grade Essential Skills Inventory

Reading

- Uses phonics knowledge to decode words in context
- Recognizes basic sight words
- Reads with fluency
- Reads for pleasure
- Identifies story elements using reading strategies
- Identifies main ideas
- Monitors comprehension while reading
- Makes inferences when reading
- Makes text-to-text, self, world connections

Language

- Uses age-appropriate vocabulary
- Demonstrates effective listening skills
- Uses language to recognize feelings in self and others

Writing

- Prints neatly and writes neatly in cursive
- Spells using visual memory
- Spells using phonics skills and word patterns
- Uses capitalization and punctuation
- Writes a paragraph using full sentences
- Expresses a clear opinion in oral and written form
- Edits and revises drafts

Mathematics

- Reads and writes numbers to 10,000 in words and numerals
- Uses common units of measurement: Length, weight, time, money, and temperature
- Can add or subtract three-digit problems on paper with regrouping
- Can round numbers to the 10s
- Can round numbers to the 100s
- Add and subtract two-digit numbers mentally
- Counts by 5, 6, 7, 8, 9 and 10 using manipulatives
- Uses arrays to visually depict multiplication
- Recognizes basic fractions
- Solves written and oral story problems using the correct operation

Behavior

- Shows interest in learning
- Demonstrates empathy for fellow students

Organization

- Organizes to complete a task in school
- Organizes to complete a task at home

D. ESSENTIAL SKILLS RUBRIC FOR FIRST GRADE

	Intervention	Developing	Proficient
Letters			
Identifies uppercase letters	Identifies fewer than 15 uppercase letters	Identifies 16–25 uppercase letters	Automatically identifies all uppercase letters
Identifies lowercase letters	Identifies fewer than 15 lowercase letters	Identifies 16–25 lowercase letters	Automatically identifies all lowercase letters
Phonological Skills			
Identifies a sound associated with each letter	Knows fewer than 15 letter sounds	Knows 15–20 letter sounds	Knows 20 or more letter sounds
Produces rhymes for a given word	Unable to produce a rhyme	Can produce real-word rhymes for a given word	Can produce real-or nonsense-word rhymes for a given word
Identifies beginning, middle, ending sounds	Can identify beginning sound of spoken word, but confuses or doesn't hear middle and ending sounds	Usually able to identify beginning and ending sounds of spoken words	Able to identify beginning, middle, and ending sounds of words
Combines phonemes to make words	Unable to blend segmented sounds into words	With prompting or assistance, can blend segmented sounds into a word	Given segmented sounds, can blend into a word (/p/ /a/ /t/ = pat)
Language			
Uses age-appropriate vocabulary in speech	Speech is difficult to understand; has trouble understanding basic vocabulary for nouns, verbs, concepts; difficulty following more than 1-step directions	Speaks in incomplete sentences; doesn't always use or understand age-appropriate words for nouns, verbs, concepts; may have difficulty following 1- or 2-step directions	Speaks in full, grammatically correct sentences; uses and understands age-appropriate words representing nouns, verbs, concepts; understands directions
Uses language to solve problems	Uses physical means to solve problems	Needs guidance and modeling to appropriately use language to solve problems	When faced with a problem, uses language in an acceptable way to find a solution

(continued)

(continued)

	Intervention	Developing	Proficient
Demonstrates effective listening skills	Has difficulty following more than one oral direction at a time; needs frequent reminders to actively listen in large and small groups; unable to paraphrase/retell directions, discussions, etc.	Follows 2- or 3-step oral directions in a sequence; actively listens in large and small groups with minimal guidance; can paraphrase/retell directions, discussion, etc. with help	Follows 3- or 4-step oral directions in a sequence; actively listens in large and small groups; understands direction words (location, space, and time words); can paraphrase/retell directions, discussions, etc.
Motor Skills			
Demonstrates appropriate balance	Unsteady with eyes open while standing on one foot for 6 seconds	Able to stand on one foot with eyes open for 6 to 10 seconds	Able to stand on one foot with eyes closed for 6 seconds
Demonstrates appropriate skipping	Unable to skip, might gallop instead	Skip is very deliberate, requires a lot of concentration	Skips with smooth rhythm and gait for 10 yards
Uses comfortable near-point vision	Avoids prolonged use of near-point vision for reading and writing; eyes may tire when child engages near-point vision, as evidenced by rubbing eyes, shifting head to different positions, or watering eyes	Enjoys reading and writing for brief periods; eyes show signs of visual fatigue after prolonged use	Uses eyes for reading and writing activities for more than 15 minutes without distress
Visualization			
Draws pictures with detail	Drawing is primitive with very little detail	Needs prompting to add details to a picture	Draws a picture with rich detail (eyes, nose, mouth, hair, limbs, appendages, etc.)
Can tell/retell a story	Confuses story events or is unable to tell what happened	Accurately recalls story but omits one or two story elements	Accurately recalls story events with all elements present
Literacy			
Recognizes basic sight words	Recognizes less than 50% of grade-level sight words automatically	Recognizes 50–90% of grade-level sight words automatically	Recognizes 90–100% of grade-level sight words automatically

	Intervention	Developing	Proficient
Follows print when reading (visual tracking)	Has difficulty matching one-to-one (voice-print match)	Can read two lines of text tracking left to right and return sweep without losing place and without using fingers	Can read multiple lines of text tracking left to right without losing place and without using fingers
Decodes grade-appropriate print	Does not have strategies for decoding words; stops reading or asks what the unknown word is	Beginning to use letter-sound relationships to decode words (can say the sound of first letter, then may use picture clues, or may sound out letter by letter)	Uses multiple strategies (word patterns, letter-sound relationship) to decode grade-level words
Reads short sentences	Has difficulty reading short sentences	Reads short sentences, but reads word by word and makes errors	Reads short sentences accurately and fluently
Reads for meaning	Is unaware of reading errors	Self-monitors reading but needs guidance to correct errors	Uses context clues; self-monitors and self-corrects
Prints 30 to 50 personally meaningful words	Prints fewer than 10 meaningful words	Prints 10–29 meaningful words	Prints 30–50 meaningful words
Expresses ideas in writing (simple sentences)	Has difficulty composing a complete sentence	Able to compose 1 or 2 simple sentences	Can independently compose 2 or 3 simple sentences
Spells using common word patterns	Spells mostly phonetically; doesn't use word families or known rhyme patterns to spell new words	Spells some words using word family or rhyme patterns, but may need prompting: "If you know . . . , then you can spell . . ."	Correctly and independently spells words using common word family or rhyme patterns
Spells words using visual memory	Frequently misspells age-appropriate high-frequency words	Spells most high-frequency grade-level words accurately	Spells high-frequency grade level words accurately
Numeracy			
Counts objects with accuracy to 100	Counts fewer than 20 objects with accuracy	Sometimes counts objects with accuracy (to 100)	Consistently counts objects with accuracy (to 100)
Replicates visual patterns or movement patterns	Has difficulty replicating a 2-step visual pattern (i.e., square-circle, red-blue) or a 2-step movement pattern (i.e., clap hands, step forward)	Can sometimes replicate a 2- or 3-step visual or movement pattern	Can consistently replicate a 3-step or 4-step visual pattern or movement pattern

(continued)

(continued)

	Intervention	Developing	Proficient
Recognizes number groups without counting (2–10)	Recognizes number groups without counting (to 3)	Sometimes recognizes number groups without counting (to 10)	Consistently recognizes number groups without counting (to 10)
Understands concepts of add on or take away (to 30) with manipulates	Unable to add on or take away numbers from a group (to 10)	Using an abacus (or other standard counting manipulative), can add on or take away numbers from group, but must recount to find resulting number (to 30)	Using an abacus (or other standard counting manipulative), can add on or take away numbers and name resulting number (to 30)
Can add or subtract single-digit problems on paper	Needs assistance to add single digit problems on paper	Adds single digit problems on paper independently but with partial accuracy	Adds single digit problems on paper independently and accurately
Shows a group of objects by number (to 100)	Can show fewer than 20 objects by number	Sometimes shows objects by number (to 100)	Consistently shows objects by number (to 100)
Behavior			
Delays gratification when necessary	Unable to delay gratification without becoming upset	Can delay gratification with encouragement or prompting	Can independently delay gratification when needed
Plays well with others	Often has difficulty engaging in cooperative play without adult assistance	With minimal prompts or modeling, can participate in cooperative play successfully	Participates in cooperative play successfully (kind words, takes turns, shares)
Shows interest in learning	Is often off-task; seems disinterested in topic of study; creates distractions during group work or instruction time	Is sometimes off-task; interest in topic of study is unpredictable; will contribute to group when asked for input	Can follow instructions independently; completes work on time; makes contributions to group lessons

E. PROTOCOL FOR USE OF THE
ESSENTIAL SKILLS INVENTORIES IN K–3

The Essential Skills Inventories (ESIs) (K–3) are a simple format for assessing the most important skills in the development of language, literacy, numeracy, motor skill, and behavior and social skills during the first years of school. They serve as a universal screening and progress monitoring tool. More importantly, they are an ongoing formative assessment tool for teachers.

Teachers are encouraged to observe students during typical instructional activities during the first 6 weeks of school. Through this observational phase, teachers collect baseline data.

Once this information is collected, teachers use the data regarding student skills and needs to plan instruction. Teachers will now have a clear picture of which students have or do not yet have important skills. They now refer to this information as they formulate weekly or daily lesson plans.

Two sections of ESI are updated each week. This might mean that during one week, the teachers will update observation of progress toward proficiency in two of the seven to eight major sections of the inventory.

Student proficiency is noted only after the student has demonstrated this skill at the proficient level on several occasions and in different uses or contexts. To determine proficiency, teachers use multiple points of observation, within several different contexts, to ensure solid skills.

A date is entered on the ESI to indicate proficiency.

The principal will meet with grade-level teachers or individual teachers monthly to review the progress of students. These monthly data review meetings are important for building the routine of formative assessment and responsive instruction.

Data from the ESI are considered when making referrals to the school's Support Team.

Individual student data can be used for communication with parents. The individual student data form allows teachers to rate student progress as Intervention, Developing, or Proficient. Classroom data are never be used for individual discussions.

The goal is to help at least 90% of all students reach proficiency in every skill by the end of the school year.

© Early Learning Foundation

PROTOCOL FOR USE OF THE ESSENTIAL SKILLS INVENTORIES IN K–3

1. Collect baseline data during the first 6 weeks of school.

2. Use data regarding student skills and needs to plan instruction.

3. Update two sections of the ESI each week.

4. Review data with principal monthly.

5. Proficiency will be noted only after the student has demonstrated this skill at the proficient level on several occasions and in different uses or contexts.

6. A date will be entered on the ESI to indicate proficiency.

7. Data will be considered when making referrals to the Support Team.

8. Individual student data can be used for communication with parents. Classroom data should not be used for individual discussions.

9. Our goal is to help at least 90% of our students reach proficiency in every skill by the end of the school year.

F. QUESTIONS AND TOPICS
FOR MONTHLY DATA MEETINGS

Which sections of the Essential Skills Inventory did you update last week?

How did you collect your baseline data? Did other staff members help?

Are you able to build assessment into instructional activities, or do you construct separate assessment activities?

How did you assess _____?

What are you going to do with your knowledge of the varied skill levels in math?

What are you going to do with your knowledge of the varied skill levels in language?

Which students need intensive support in developing behavior skills?

Which students need intensive support in developing phonologic skills?

Do you have math center activities you could share with other grade-level teachers?

Do you have small group math activities you could share with other grade-level teachers?

Are there children for whom you need extra help or support?

Are there materials or services you need?

Which two sections of the inventory are you assessing this week?

Is it difficult to get into the routine of updating your classroom data weekly?

G. REFLECTION ON CLASSROOM CULTURE

In our classrooms, we recognize that children learn best when they feel safe, connected to the teacher and their classmates, and competent to succeed in learning and life. This reflection is to help us refine the ideas and practices that support this belief.

Rate yourself on a scale of 0 to 5, with 5 representing the goal of consistent application of this skill or idea.

Each day I greet children with warmth and empathy.	_____
We begin the day with a consistent routine.	_____
Children have learned all essential procedures to mastery.	_____
Each day I am conscious of the need to develop and maintain empathetic connections with my students, especially the neediest students.	_____
Before I set a limit on student behavior or impose a consequence, I always pause to build the empathetic connection.	_____
Sometimes I choose to delay consequences.	_____
The children in my classroom absolutely know what good behavior in our classroom looks like and support this standard.	_____
Sometimes I choose to offer students choices.	_____
Usually I encourage students to solve their own problems.	_____
I am very aware of the instructional levels and needs of my students and make adjustments in my lessons to allow each student to have three or four chunks of time at the correct instructional level each day.	_____
Kids feel safe in my classroom.	_____
I love the culture in my classroom.	_____
Most of the time, I can smile when a child makes a poor behavior choice, knowing that he/she is about to have an important learning opportunity.	_____

H. REFLECTION ON SCHOOL CULTURE

> In our school, we recognize that students learn best, teachers teach best, and parents offer the greatest support when they feel safe, connected, and competent. This reflection is to help principals refine the ideas and practices that support this belief.

Rate yourself or the staff on a scale of 0 to 5, with 5 representing the goal of consistent application of this skill or idea.

Each day I greet students with warmth and empathy.	_____
Each day I greet staff with warmth and empathy.	_____
Students understand all essential procedures in our school.	_____
Our staff understands all essential procedures in our school.	_____
Each day I am conscious of the need to develop and maintain empathetic connections with students, especially the neediest students.	_____
Each day I work to build trusting professional connections with other educators in our school.	_____
I consciously build relationships with parents.	_____
Before I set a limit on behavior or impose a consequence, I always pause to build the empathetic connection.	_____
Sometimes I choose to delay consequences.	_____
Sometimes I choose to offer choices.	_____
Usually I encourage students and staff to solve their own problems.	_____
I choose to consider the individual situations and needs of each student when I deal with behavior infractions. Sometimes that allows people to question my decisions and creates more work, but I do it anyway.	_____
Parents feel respected and valued every time they have contact with our school.	_____
Kids feel safe in our school.	_____
Staff demonstrates collaboration skills.	_____
Staff recognizes that asking for support is both encouraged and respected.	_____
I love the culture in our school.	_____
Most of the time, I can smile when a child makes a poor behavior choice, knowing that he/she is about to have an important learning opportunity.	_____

I. REFLECTION ON HOME–SCHOOL CONNECTIONS

We recognize the importance of home–school connections and purposely build trusting relationships with the parents/guardians of our students. This reflection is to help us refine the ideas and practices that support this belief.

Rate yourself on a scale of 0 to 5, with 5 representing the goal of consistent application of this skill or idea.

Building trusting relationships with parents is a priority with me.	_____
I ask parents to tell me about their children and any special hopes or goals they have for this year.	_____
I quickly learn the names of my students and their family members.	_____
I communicate frequently with parents.	_____
I return calls/e-mails promptly.	_____
I make 2–5 purely positive communications about my students' learning and behavior each week.	_____
I go out of my way to build relationships with struggling parents.	_____
I invite parents to do meaningful volunteer work in my classroom.	_____
I have a lending library available to parents.	_____
I carefully prepare for meetings/conferences with parents.	_____
In meetings with parents, I have learned to listen more than I talk.	_____
I offer advice or solutions only after parents are in a calm, problem-solving state of mind.	_____
I try to have interactions with parents in which they have a positive emotional experience that builds closer ties with our school.	_____

J. REFLECTION ON THE EARLY LEARNING SUCCESS INITIATIVE IN OUR SCHOOL

Identify the strengths and weaknesses of your school's early learning success initiative to date.

Caring, Connected Classroom and School Culture

1. Each day staff members greet children with warmth and empathy.

2. Each classroom begins the day with a consistent routine.

3. Children have learned/are learning all essential procedures to mastery.

4. Before staff set limits on student behavior, or impose consequences for poor choices, they always pause to build an empathetic connection.

5. Children absolutely know what good behavior looks like in the classroom, hallways, lunchroom, playground, and support this standard.

6. Teachers are aware of the instructional levels and needs of their students, and plan lessons in keeping with this knowledge.

7. Staff reach out to parents, create positive emotional experiences for parents, and build trusting relationships.

8. Staff builds trusting relationships among themselves to support schoolwide collaboration, procedures, and positive culture.

Use of Universal Screening and Progress Monitoring to Understand What Children Know and Are Ready to Learn

1. Teachers consistently use a simple, efficient progress monitoring tool, which allows daily consideration of progress toward all essential skills, including language, phonologic, literacy, numeracy, sensory-motor, behavioral, and social skills.

2. Essential data are updated weekly and lead to the design and delivery of classroom instruction that meets the needs of students.

3. Support is available to teachers who struggle to collect essential data.

4. Additional formative assessment tools are available when a more careful assessment of a specific aspect of learning is needed.

A Team Is Available to Respond to Teacher Requests for Support

1. Teachers understand and support the idea that helping children experience early learning success is far preferable to allowing children to struggle in the early years of school. They are committed to developing a system that supports early learning success for every possible learner.

2. Teachers clearly understand the process of requesting support for student(s) who are not making optimal progress.

3. Response to a teacher request occurs quickly, within the guidelines of the support team process.

4. Case managers clarify teacher requests for support, and include other helping staff as needed.

5. A record-keeping system for instructional support is clearly defined.

6. Case managers follow a defined process for long-term collaboration.

7. Case managers respect the classroom teacher as the primary provider of service to the student, and the person who knows what interventions are possible within the classroom.

8. Support interactions are always professional. Meetings are on time. Staff members use available time and resources wisely.

9. Support plans are specific and measurable.

10. Successes are celebrated.

Quality Classroom Instruction

1. Teachers use consistent routines in their classrooms.

2. Teachers have developed a culture of respect and safety in the classroom.

3. Essential early learning outcomes have been clearly defined in all aspects of skill development.

4. K–3 teachers monitor growth toward essential outcomes and use this information to plan instruction. The essential outcome inventories are updated weekly.

5. Teachers have developed a variety of skills to support differentiated instruction.

6. Teachers offer instruction at the level of student readiness for the development of all essential skills.

NOTES:

K. SAMPLE DISTRICT PLAN FOR
EARLY LEARNING SUCCESS

The _____ School District has made a long-term commitment to becoming a district that uses formative assessment and offers responsive instruction. We will help students establish deep understanding of essential content and will meet the needs of our students by designing instruction at their levels of readiness. To this end we will establish and implement a 3-year to 5-year plan to develop the teaching skills and systems that supports these goals.

The plan described in this document focuses on the steps toward implementation at the elementary schools in our district and describes Year 1 of the long-term training commitment to early learning success.

ELEMENTARY OUTCOMES

1. We will have a system of universal screening and progress monitoring, which defines essential outcomes, in all elementary schools.

2. Teachers will develop skills to deliver instruction well-matched to the learning needs of students.

3. An accountability system will be fully implemented in all schools to support proper implementation.

4. A system of instructional support will be implemented in each elementary building, with clear procedures and time lines.

5. A culture of professional trust and collaboration will be explicitly defined and established in each school.

6. An ongoing plan for professional learning to support learning success for all children will be developed and implemented.

Outcome #1: We will have a K–3 system of universal screening and progress monitoring, which defines essential outcomes, in all elementary schools.

Discussion

The system should be simple, align with the report card, encourage us to take the time to help students deeply learn essential outcomes, help more students be successful, remind us to take time for social skill development, reduce anxiety, and increase joy. It should help us have fewer special education referrals and help us have more support time available for general education.

1. Training in the use of the Essential Skills Inventory will be given to K–3 teachers before the beginning of the school year.

    Action Plan: The Curriculum Director will arrange for dates and trainer.

2. Clarify how this information and process may be used.
    - Compliance with the protocol for data collection is expected of all classroom teachers and can be considered a factor in evaluation.
    - Essential Skill proficiency will be noted only after the student has demonstrated this skill at the proficient level on several occasions and in different uses or contexts.

    Action Plan: Principals will monitor progress in monthly data meetings.

3. A committee will develop a process to align the report card with the Essential Skills Inventories.

    Action Plan: A study team will be appointed in May and will review and report to the Curriculum Director by August.

4. A clear directive from central office will describe the district's commitment to using essential skills as a focus for responsive instruction.

> *The _____ Public Schools are committed to using instructional strategies that maximize learning outcomes and encourages teachers to use techniques to deliver instruction that is responsive to student readiness. We recognize that students will be at different levels of readiness within a single class and that teachers will need to differentiate instruction at times within their classrooms to meet the learning needs of students. Teachers will deliver a rich instructional program that includes grade-level content and purposeful activities and projects and will also vigilantly monitor progress toward essential skills and outcomes. Pacing guides are to be used as guides. Students needing additional time or intensive practice to learn essential outcomes will be given that time and support.*

Action Plan: The District Superintendent and the Board of Education will pass a motion to this effect by August.

5. Teachers at each grade level (K–3) will develop a plan for integrating use of any typical assessment tools, that is, DRA or MLPP, with the ESI.

    Action Plan: A study team will be appointed in May and will review and report to the Curriculum Director by August.

6. A plan will be developed for keeping data on file within each school and sharing info with next year's teacher.

    Action Plan: Building teams will prepare a plan and report to the Curriculum Director by December.

7. Midyear follow-up training in use of the Essential Skills Inventory will be given to teachers in Grades K–3.

    Action Plan: The Curriculum Director will arrange for dates and trainer.

8. Addition training needs to help teachers learn skills to help more students achieve all essential outcomes will be specifically noted, considered, and planned.

    Action Plan: Building Principals will collect input on learning needs, and a long-term plan will be developed in conjunction with the Curriculum Director by March.

Outcome #2: Teachers will develop skills to deliver instruction well matched to the learning needs of students.

1. Grade-level teachers will collaborate to support each other in the development of assessment procedures for essential skills and responsive instructional planning.

   Action Plan: Building Principals will offer support to grade-level staff and schedule time for them to collaborate.

2. Learning needs will be noted and professional development planned.

   Action Plan: Building Principals will collect input on learning needs, and a long-term plan will be developed in conjunction with the Curriculum Director by March.

Outcome #3: An accountability system will be fully implemented in all schools to support proper implementation of the Essential Skills Inventory.

1. The Protocol for Use of the Essential Skills Inventory will be followed in K–3.

   Action Plan: Building Principals will meet with teachers by grade level or individually monthly.

2. Progress toward quality formative assessment will be reported in quarterly reviews.

   Action Plan: Building Principals will offer a brief update on their progress at quarterly principal meetings. The Curriculum Director will place this on meeting agendas.

3. Support team referrals will include a review of the data from the ESI. Case managers will review this data with the referring teacher.

   Action Plan: Principals and case managers will ensure compliance.

Outcome #4: A system of instructional support will be implemented in each elementary building, with clear procedures and time lines.

Discussion

Consistent procedures and paperwork will be developed to be used in all elementary programs. Teachers must be made aware of the opportunity to request support, have simple steps to receive help, and be encouraged to collaborate without waiting for students to become severely frustrated. Guidelines for when to refer to Instructional Support Team and when to refer to Special Education will be developed.

1. Support team members will be identified.

   Action Plan: Principals will identify staff and consider time available for instructional support by August.

2. Written procedures and related forms will be developed.

   Action Plan: A committee will be appointed in May and will complete a draft proposal to the Curriculum Director and Principals by August.

3. Implementation training will be given to each school's support team, with follow-up for the first 2 years, beginning September. Initial training will be followed by three coaching days in each school for each of the first 2 years.

   Action Plan: The Curriculum Director will arrange for dates and trainer by August.

4. Each school's support team will prepare a plan to communicate the process and procedures to classroom teachers.

   Action Plan: Support teams will construct a plan and begin this process in September.

5. End-of-year data will be collected, noting the number of referrals, of what type, cases that reached closure, open cases carried over to following year, special education referrals, special education placements, etc.

   Action Plan: Principals will collect info and report to the Curriculum Director by June 15.

6. Each school's support team will complete an annual reflection on the support process.

   Action Plan: Principals will collect and discuss at the end of the year and use this input to help plan for future needs.

7. Each support team will develop a procedure for informing next year's teachers about specific children who have received intensive support.

   Action Plan: A plan will be developed by May. Principals will supervise sharing information.

8. All schools will participate in an end-of-year meeting where they will share accomplishments and identify learning goals for future consideration.

   Action Plan: The Curriculum Director and Principals will plan and coordinate an end of year meeting, to be held in May.

Outcome #5: A culture of professional trust and collaboration will be explicitly defined and established in each school.

Discussion

The collaborative culture includes clear group norms, time for communication, and the comfort to be open with staff both individually and at group meetings. Working toward this collaborative culture will include bonding and team building activities, development of Professional Learning Communities, building and district grade-level sharing, an emphasis on quality general education/special education planning, and a building and district-level commitment to this expectation. Professional trust and collaboration will help us create the problem-solving and learning environment that improves instructional planning, building the culture of learning for students, and building the culture of support for parents.

1. Each school will consider the importance of a collaborative culture and establish group norms for the collaborative culture.

   Action Plan: A survey of perceptions of school culture will be prepared and shared with staff at the beginning of the school year. Principals will have a discussion about the importance of collaborative culture at a staff

meeting(s) early in the year and ask for commitment from each individual once group norms have been reached by consensus. This process will begin in September.

2. A reflection on individual teacher use of the group norms will be developed and used quarterly to support the development of the collaborative culture.

   Action Plan: A teacher leadership team will be selected by the Principal to develop this instrument. The building Principal will distribute the reflection to teachers quarterly.

3. Teachers will discuss the results of their self-reflection at building grade-level meetings.

   Action Plan: Teachers will schedule this discussion after each self-reflection quarterly.

4. The principal will survey perceptions of school culture at the end of the school year.

   Action Plan: Principals will review progress at summer council.

Outcome #6: An ongoing system of professional learning to support learning success for all children will be developed and implemented in all schools.

Discussion

An effective ongoing system of professional learning will include a clear understanding of common learning goals for our students, and common teaching skills and strategies that can support the achievement of these learning outcomes. When we have identified core teaching skills/ strategies that each teacher should have, we can identify teachers to serve as mentor teachers and can also identify teachers who need support to develop these skills. We strive to develop an ongoing learning process within our collaborative culture. Training opportunities should be differentiated and available based on the need of individual teachers in addition to recognizing group needs for whole group learning. At the district and building levels, important learning initiatives should be clearly identified and supported over time to achieve quality, ongoing implementation.

1. Learning needs to support districtwide initiatives will be identified annually, and a plan to train staff will be developed for the following year.

   Action Plan: A committee including the Curriculum Director, Principals, and teacher leaders will coordinate, with input from staff. A plan for the following year will be developed by March for implementation in the summer and the following school year.

2. The planning committee will do research and develop a set of teaching skills that support the full implementation of an early learning success initiative. These skills will be part of the focus of professional development.

   Action Plan: The committee will convene in October and begin work toward identifying common teaching skills needed for K–3 early learning success. Once identified, these skills will be incorporated into the long term training plan. The long-term training program will include considerations for training existing staff, training new staff, developing mentor programs within staff, and sharing materials to support this initiative. The Curriculum Director will convene the planning committee and oversee this process.

L. SAMPLE SUPPORT TEAM PROCEDURES

Tier 1

The classroom teacher is responsible for delivering a rich and interesting curriculum, and for designing instruction to help each student become proficient in each of the essential skills. Teachers will adjust instruction and differentiate instruction to accomplish these outcomes. Informal collaboration among staff is encouraged.

Tier 2

Referral Process

For students whose learning/behavior needs require additional services, teachers will follow these Instructional Support procedures. Teachers are encouraged to ask for assistance, including the following: short-term consultation; long-term collaborative problem solving; material or technology accommodation; developing an accommodation plan; constructing a behavior plan; behavior management coaching; short-term coteaching support; and other needs as determined appropriate.

1. Teachers will complete the **Teacher Request for Instructional Support** form and the **Classroom Intervention Documentation** form, and turn it in to the **principal.**

2. The teacher will receive confirmation that her/his request has been received, and the **principal** will assign a **case manager**.

3. Within 2 school days, the **case manager** will contact the teacher to set up an initial meeting with the classroom teacher or to plan service.

4. At this meeting between the **case manager and classroom teacher,** specific outcomes and steps toward these outcomes will be identified. Parents will be notified by the teacher before services begin.

5. The **case manager** is responsible for managing the paperwork and establishing a file for each case.

Instructional Support Team

1. A corps of **case managers** will be selected, with specific time available to consult with teachers and provide follow-up services clearly identified.

2. Cases will be assigned by the **principal**, based on training and experience dealing with learning/behavioral issues.

3. **Case managers** will make contact with the requesting classroom teacher within 2 school days of the request, clarify the specific nature of the request, and begin consultation with the teacher.

4. Requesting K–3 teachers will have up-to-date Essential Skill data, and other information as needed, to establish baseline for progress monitoring that will be a part of the plan.

5. The **case manager** is responsible for managing the appropriate paperwork and establishing a file for each case.

6. Every meeting with the teacher and the **case manager** will include establishing a plan for follow-up until closure is achieved for that case.

7. Support team **case managers** will meet biweekly with the principal for a case review meeting. This meeting will be a brief review of the status of each referral, specifically noting the nature of the request, action taken, and progress noted. **Case managers** will ask for help from the team if warranted.

8. Additional Instructional Support Team (IST) members will be identified as available for consultation in certain cases, that is, if a sensory-motor screening is needed the Occupational Therapist may be consulted. These members will not attend the biweekly case review meetings unless specifically requested.

Instructional Support Team Files

1. Case managers will maintain active files.

2. A file space in the office will be designated for all inactive/closed files.

3. A summary of results will be placed in all closed files, which will be stored in the office file.

4. At the end of each year, each case manager will give a summary of all cases, open and closed, to the principal.

5. The CA60 of each student referred to IST will be designated with a blue dot, indicating that the IST file is available for review by a subsequent teacher.

© Early Learning Foundation

6. The IST file for all students moving to middle schools will be shared with the middle school principal.

7. A list of all students with active IST case files will be shared with the following year's teacher, who will review the file and observe student progress before reactivating the case or requesting closure.

Tier 3

1. Tier 1 and 2 interventions will be reviewed by the Multidisciplinary Evaluation Team to support the decision regarding whether to move to formal evaluation.

2. For students whose learning/behavioral needs meet the threshold for special education referral/placement, district and county special education guidelines will be followed.

M. TEACHER REQUEST FOR INSTRUCTIONAL SUPPORT

Student: _____   Date of Birth: _____

Teacher: _____   Grade: _____

School: _____   Date of Request: _____

Statement of Concern:

Best Times for Me to Meet:

Support Requested:

- ❑ Short-term consultation with a member of the building support team
- ❑ Collaborative problem solving (long-term)
- ❑ Materials or technology to allow accommodation for this child's learning needs
- ❑ Developing an accommodation plan
- ❑ Constructing a behavior plan
- ❑ Classroom behavior management coaching
- ❑ Small-group counseling support for this student
- ❑ Sensory-motor needs assessment
- ❑ Co-teaching support
- ❑ An extended learning-time option for this student
- ❑ Literacy assessment/support for this student
- ❑ Math/numeracy assessment/support program for this student
- ❑ Other:

Notes:

N. PREK–GRADE 3 ESSENTIAL MATH SKILLS INVENTORY

Bob Sornson, PhD, Early Learning Foundation

(PreK) Demonstrates one-to-one correspondence for numbers 1–10, with steps

(PreK) Demonstrates one-to-one correspondence for numbers 1–10, with manipulatives

(PreK) Adds on/takes away using numbers 1–10, with steps

(PreK) Adds on/takes away using numbers 1–10, with manipulatives

(K) Demonstrates counting to 100

(K) Has one-to-one correspondence for numbers 1–30

(K) Understands combinations (to 10)

(K) Recognizes number groups without counting (2–10)

(1) Understands concepts of add on or take away (to 30)

(1) Adds/subtracts single digit problems on paper

(1) Counts objects with accuracy to 100

(1) Replicates visual or movement patterns

(1) Shows a group of objects by number (to 100)

(2) Quickly recognizes number groups (to 100)

(2) Adds/subtracts from a group of objects (to 100)

(2) Adds/subtracts double digit problems on paper

(2) Counts by 2, 3, 4, 5, and 10 using manipulatives

(2) Solves written and oral story problems using the correct operations

(2) Understands/identifies place value to 1,000

(3) Reads and writes numbers to 10,000 in words and numerals

(3) Uses common units of measurement:

- Length
- Weight
- Time
- Money
- Temperature

(3) Can add or subtract three digit problems on paper with regrouping

(3) Can round numbers to the 10s

(3) Can round numbers to the 100s

(3) Add and subtract two-digit numbers mentally

(3) Counts by 5, 6, 7, 8, 9, 10 using manipulatives

(3) Uses arrays to visually depict multiplication

(3) Recognizes basic fractions

(3) Solves written and oral story problems using the correct operation

Student: _____		Teacher: _____		Date: _____
Skill	**Not Yet**	**Intervention**	**Developing**	**Proficient**
Demonstrates one-to-one correspondence for numbers 1–10, with steps				
Demonstrates one-to-one correspondence for numbers 1–10, with manipulatives				
Adds on using numbers 1–10, with steps				
Adds on using numbers 1–10, with manipulatives				
Demonstrates counting to 100				
Has one-to-one correspondence for numbers 1–30				
Understands combinations (to 10)				
Recognizes number groups without counting (2–10)				
Understands concepts of add on or take away (to 30)				
Adds/subtracts single digit problems on paper				
Counts objects with accuracy to 100				
Replicates visual or movement patterns				
Shows a group of objects by number (to 100)				
Quickly recognizes number groups (to 100)				
Adds/subtracts from a group of objects (to 100)				
Adds/subtracts double-digit problems on paper				
Counts by 2, 3, 4, 5, and 10 using manipulatives				
Solves written and oral story problems using the correct operations				
Understands/identifies place value to 1,000				

Skill	Not Yet	Intervention	Developing	Proficient
Reads and writes numbers to 10,000 in words and numerals				
Uses common units of measurement:				
• Length				
• Weight				
• Time				
• Money				
• Temperature				
Can add or subtract three-digit problems on paper with regrouping				
Can round numbers to the 10s				
Can round numbers to the 100s				
Add and subtract two-digit numbers mentally				
Counts by 5, 6, 7, 8, 9, 10 using manipulatives				
Uses arrays to visually depict multiplication				
Recognizes basic fractions				
Solves written and oral story problems using the correct operation				

O. BUILDING ESSENTIAL SKILLS: PARENT SUPPORT REQUEST

Dear Parent,

We are committed to helping your child build all the skills in the early grades that predict long-term learning success. Attached you will find a list of Essential Skills that we are working on this year. During the year, we will vigilantly monitor your child's progress toward proficiency in every one of these skills. As soon as your child is proficient in a skill, we will move on to more advanced skills. But this list reminds us of the skills that must be carefully and fully developed.

And we could use your help. Following, we have identified two or three skills we'd like you to help your child develop this marking period. By working on these skills, you will be helping us, and more importantly helping your child, reach these essential skills as soon as possible. By next marking period, we might have a different set of skills for which we will ask for help, but right now, these are the skills that need some extra practice time at home.

Thank you so much for your support. Working together, we can help your child build a solid foundation of learning skills that will make learning fun and predict long-term success.

Sincerely,

_____ Date: _____

Skill:

Specific practice activities at home:

1.

2.

Time recommended:

Make sure you have fun while doing this work with your child! Early learning
success will help your child fall in love with learning.

Skill:

Specific practice activities at home:

1.

2.

Time recommended:

Make sure you have fun while doing this work with your child! Early learning
success will help your child fall in love with learning.

Skill:

Specific practice activities at home:

1.

2.

Time recommended:

Make sure you have fun while doing this work with your child! Early learning
success will help your child fall in love with learning.

P. ESSENTIAL SKILLS INVENTORY: FIRST GRADE

Teacher: Mrs. Peterson   Baseline Data

Indicate mastery by writing mastery date to the right of the student's name and under the feature mastered

Area of Assessment	Letters		Phonologic Skills				Language			Motor Skills			Visualization		
Essential Skills	1	2	3	4	5	6	7	8	9	10	11	12	13	14	15
Student Name	Identifies uppercase letters	Identifies lowercase letters	Identifies a letter sound associated with each letter	Produces rhymes for a given word	Identifies beginning, middle, and ending sounds of words	Combines phonemes to make words	Uses age-appropriate vocabulary in speech	Uses language to solve problems	Demonstrates effective listening skills	Demonstrates appropriate balance	Demonstrates appropriate skipping	Uses comfortable near-point vision	Draws pictures with detail	Can tell or retell a story	Recognizes basic sight words
Phillip	9–28	9–28	10–3	10–20	10–26	10–26	10–1	10–25	10–26	10–1	10–1	10–1	12–7	10–15	11–2
Jimmy	9–28	10–8	10–15	10–15	12–5	12–5	3–9	10–14	10–14	11–16	12–20	11–16	12–7	10–20	1–7
Sarah	9–28	9–28	10–3	10–20	10–26	10–26	10–1	10–2	10–2	10–1	10–1	10–1	10–18	10–15	11–2
Abigail	10–15	10–30	11–7	10–15	12–5	12–5	11–9	10–14	10–14	12–20	12–20	12–20	12–7	1–21	1–7
Kendra	10–15	10–15	10–15	11–7	12–5	12–5	12–12	3–3	10–18	11–16	10–1	10–1	12–7	10–18	11–2
Danny	9–28	9–28	11–7	3–3	10–26	3–3	2–18	3–3	10–14	12–20	12–20	1–21	3–9	10–18	4–22
Junie	10–30	11–21	1–15	11–7	12–5	3–3	4–11	3–3	3–3	12–20	12–20	1–21	3–9	4–18	5–9
Justin	9–28	9–28	1–15	1–15	12–5	1–15	4–11	4–29	4–11	12–20	12–20	1–21	3–9	4–18	4–22
Tyrel	10–30	10–30	1–15	12–5	12–5	4–13		3–3		12–20	12–20	1–21	3–9	4–30	
Peter	9–28	9–28	1–15	1–15	12–5	1–15	2–18	12–12	12–12	10–18	11–16	11–16	12–7	12–7	11–2
Cassandra	9–28	9–28	11–7	11–7	12–5	1–15	12–12	12–12	10–14	10–18	11–16	11–16	10–18	1–21	11–2
Jessica	10–7	10–23	10–23	12–5	12–5	12–5				4–29			10–29	4–29	
Suzie	9–28	9–28	10–15	11–7	10–26	12–5	12–12	2–18	10–26	10–1	11–16	10–1	10–16	11–18	11–2
Ralph	9–28	9–28	10–15	11–7	10–26	12–5	12–12	6–4	3–3	10–1	11–16	10–1	12–7	12–7	11–2
Joel	9–28	9–28	10–15	1–15	12–5	1–15	4–11	3–3	1–15	11–16	10–1	11–16	3–9	4–18	11–2
Jason	9–28	9–28	10–15	11–7	12–5	12–5	12–12	6–4	1–15	12–20	12–20	1–21	12–7	12–7	4–22
Justin	9–28	9–28	10–15	10–15	10–26	12–5	12–12	3–3	6–3	10–1	10–1	11–16	10–16	12–7	11–2
Samantha	9–28	9–28	10–3	10–15	10–26	12–5	12–12	12–12	1–15	10–1	10–1	11–16	10–16	11–18	3–9
Andrew	9–28	9–28	10–15	11–7	12–5	1–15	2–18	12–12	1–15	12–20	12–20	12–7	12–7	12–7	1–7
Marcus	9–28	9–28	10–15	2–2	12–5	1–15	4–11	12–12	3–3	12–20	12–20	1–21	3–9	1–21	4–22
Dylan	9–28	9–28	10–15	3–3	12–5	3–3	4–11	6–4	12–12	10–1	11–16	11–16	3–9	11–18	6–4
Camilla	9–28	9–28	10–3	10–15	10–26	11–7	11–9	11–9	10–14	10–1	10–1	10–1	10–16	11–18	11–2
Katie	9–28	9–28	10–3	10–15	10–26	11–7	11–9	11–9	10–14	10–1	10–1	10–1	10–16	11–18	11–2
Leroy	11–6	11–6	11–6	11–6	11–6	1–15	11–9	11–9	1–15	11–16	11–16	11–16	12–7	12–7	2–19

	Literacy								Numeracy						Behavior		
	16	17	18	19	20	21	22	23	24	25	26	27	28	29	30	31	32
	Follows print when reading (visual tracking)	Decodes grade-appropriate print	Reads short sentences	Reads for meaning	Prints 30 to 50 personally meaningful words	Expresses ideas in writing (simple sentences)	Spells using common word patterns	Spells words using visual memory	Counts objects with accuracy to 100	Replicates visual patterns or movement patterns	Recognizes number groups without counting (2 to 10)	Understands concepts of add on or take away (to 30) with manipulatives	Adds/subtracts single digit problems on paper	Shows a group of objects by number (to 100)	Delays gratification when necessary	Plays well with others	Shows interest in learning
10–18	10–4	10–18	12–5	10–4	10–4	10–18	1–9	10–22	10–19	9–25	11–10	10–6	11–10	10–15	2–2	10–1
1–7	1–7	1–7	2–19	2–19	4–11	2–19	4–22	11–10	11–10	10–14	2–6	11–10	2–6	10–8	10–5	10–1
10–18	10–4	10–18	12–5	10–4	10–4	10–18	1–9	10–25	10–19	9–14	11–10	10–6	11–10	10–1	10–5	10–1
1–7	1–7	1–7	2–19	3–16	3–16	4–11	5–12	11–10	11–10	11–10	4–29	11–10	2–6	11–29	11–29	3–19
10–18	11–4	11–4	12–5	1–7	12–5	12–5	1–9	2–6	11–10	10–14	12–1	11–10	12–1	10–8	10–5	10–5
1–7	1–7	1–7	2–19	3–16	3–16	4–22	4–22	10–26	11–10	11–10	4–29	11–10	3–14	10–15	2–2	11–29
1–7	1–7	1–7	2–19	3–16	3–16	4–29	5–16	2–6	2–6	11–10	4–29	4–29	4–29	11–29	1–9	2–2
1–7	1–7	1–7	4–22	3–16	3–16	4–22	4–22	10–26	11–10	11–10	4–20	11–10	3–14	10–15	11–29	4–29
1–7	1–7	1–7	4–22	3–16	3–16			10–26	11–10	11–10	3–23	11–10	2–6	11–29	11–29	2–2
10–18	10–25	11–4	12–5	1–7	12–5	12–5	1–9	10–25	10–19	9–14	2–6	11–10	2–6	10–15	11–29	11–29
10–18	10–25	11–4	2–19	4–22	12–5	12–5	1–9	10–22	10–19	9–25	4–29	5–22	5–18	10–15	10–15	11–29
10–18	1–7	1–7	2–19	4–22				2–6	5–22	3–14	5–22	4–29	4–29	2–2	4–20	3–19
10–18	10–18	11–4	2–19	10–8	10–8	10–18	1–9	10–22	10–19	9–25	11–10	11–10	11–10	11–29	4–29	11–29
10–18	11–4	1–7	1–7	3–16	3–16	4–22		10–22	10–11	10–14	4–29	11–10	3–14	2–2	11–29	3–19
1–7	1–7	11–4	2–19	4–22	5–9	4–22	4–22	10–22	11–10	9–25	4–29	11–10	3–14	2–2	5–11	10–5
1–7	1–7	1–7	4–22	3–16	3–16	6–7	6–7	10–22	11–10	9–25	4–29	11–10	4–29	4–20	4–20	6–2
10–18	10–4	10–18	12–5	10–8	10–8	10–18	1–9	10–22	10–19	9–25	11–10	10–6	11–10	10–1	6–2	10–5
10–18	1–7	1–7	1–7	2–19	3–16	4–22	4–22	10–22	10–19	10–14	4–29	11–10	2–6	10–1	11–29	6–2
1–7	1–7	1–7	4–22	3–16	3–16	4–22	4–22	10–22	10–19	10–14	12–1	11–10	12–1	11–29	11–29	3–19
1–7	1–7	1–7	4–22	4–22	3–16	4–22	4–22	2–6	11–10	11–10	4–29	11–10	3–14	11–29	11–29	3–19
11–2	1–7	1–7	6–4	5–18	3–16	6–4	6–7	10–22	10–19	10–14	4–29	11–10	4–29	10–1	10–5	3–19
10–18	11–4	10–18	12–5	10–8	10–18	12–5	1–9	10–22	10–19	10–14	11–10	10–6	11–10	10–1	10–5	10–5
10–18	11–4	10–18	12–5	10–8	10–18	12–5	1–9	10–22	10–19	10–14	11–10	10–6	11–10	10–1	10–5	10–5
12–5	12–5	12–5	2–19	12–5	2–19	4–22	4–22	11–10	11–10	11–10	2–6	11–10	11–10	12–1	2–2	12–1

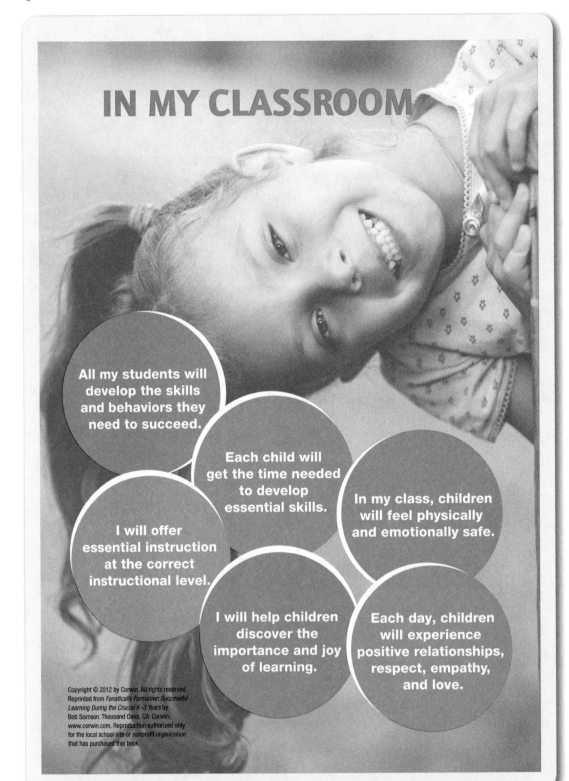

References

Chapter 1

Alexander, K. L., & Entwisle, D. R. (1988). Achievement in the first two years of school: Patterns and processes. *Monographs of the Society for Research in Child Development, 53*(2), 1–157.

Annie E. Casey Foundation. (2010), *Early warning! Why reading by the end of third grade matters.* Baltimore, MD: Author.

Barnett, W. S. (1996). *Lives in the balance: The age-27 benefit-cost analysis of the High/Scope Perry Preschool Program.* Ypsilanti, MI: High/Scope Press.

Blum, R. W., Beuhring, T., & Rinehart, P. M. (2000). *Protecting teens: Beyond race, income and family structure.* Minneapolis: University of Minnesota, Center for Adolescent Health.

Currie, J., & Duncan, T. (1995). Does Head Start make a difference? *American Economic Review, 85*(3), 341–364.

Foundation for Child Development. (2011). *PreK–3rd education.* Retrieved from http://www.fcd-us.org/our-work/prek-3rd-education

Hernandez, D. (2011). *Double jeopardy: How third-grade reading skills and poverty influence high school graduation.* Baltimore, MD: Annie E. Casey Foundation.

Miles, S., & Stipek, D. (2006). Contemporaneous and longitudinal associations between social behavior and literacy achievement in a sample of low-income elementary school children. *Child Development, 77*(1), 103–117.

National Research Council, Committee on the Prevention of Reading Difficulties in Young Children. (1998). *Preventing reading difficulties in young children.* Washington, DC: National Academy Press.

Northeastern University, Center for Labor Market Studies and Alternative Schools Network in Chicago. (2009). Left behind in America: The nation's dropout crisis. *Center for Labor Market Studies Publications.* Paper 21. Retrieved from http://hdl.handle.net/2047/d20000598.

President's Commission on Excellence in Special Education. (2002). *A new era: Revitalizing special education for children and their families.* Washington, DC: Author.

Riley, R. W., & Peterson, T. K. (2008, September 24). Before the "either-or era": Reviving bipartisanship to improve America's schools. *Education Week.*

Shaywitz, B. A., Shaywitz, S. E., Fletcher, J. M., Pugh, K. R., Gore, J. C., Constable, R. T. . . . Lacadie, C. (1997). The Yale Center for the Study of Learning and Attention: Longitudinal and neurobiological studies. *Learning Disabilities: A Multidisciplinary Journal, 8,* 21–30.

Snow, C. E., Burns, S., & Griffin, P. (Eds.) (1998). *Preventing reading difficulties in young children*. Washington, DC: National Academy Press.

Torgesen, J. K. (1998). Catch them before they fail. *American Educator, 22*(1–2), 32–39.

Tuscano, A. (1999, August/September). When schools fail children. *Our Children, The National PTA Magazine*, pp. 36–37.

U.S. Department of Education, America Reads Challenge. (1999). *Start early, finish strong: How to help every child become a reader.* Retrieved from http://www2.ed.gov/pubs/startearly/index.html

Vellutino, F. R., Scanlon, D. M., & Tanzman, M. S. (1998). The case for early intervention in diagnosing specific reading disability. *Journal of School Psychology, 36,* 367–397.

Zau, C. Z., & Betts, J. R., (2008). *Predicting success, preventing failure: An investigation of the California High School exit exam.* San Francisco, CA: Public Policy Institute of California.

Chapter 2

Allington, R. L. (2001). *What really matters for struggling readers: Designing research-based programs.* New York, NY: Longman.

Annie E. Casey Foundation. (2010). *Early warning! Why reading by the end of third grade matters.* Baltimore, MD: Author.

Betts, E. A. (1946). *Foundations of reading instruction.* New York, NY: American Book.

Clay, M. (1993). *Reading recovery: A guidebook for teachers in training.* Portsmouth, NH: Heinemann.

Clay, M. (1998). *By different paths to common outcomes.* York, ME: Stenhouse.

Educational Research Service. (2002). *Effective early reading instruction.* Arlington, VA: Author.

Fuchs, L. S., Fuchs, D., Hamlett, C. L., Hope, S. K., Hollenbeck, K. N., Capizzi, A. M., . . . Brothers, R. L. (2006). Extending responsiveness-to-intervention to math problem-solving at third grade. *Teaching Exceptional Children, 38,* 59–63.

Gickling, E. E., & Armstrong, D. L. (1978). Levels of instructional difficulty as related to on-task behavior, task completion, and comprehension. *Journal of Learning Disabilities, 11,* 32–39.

Gickling, E. E., & Rosenfield, S. (1995). Best practices in curriculum-based assessment. In A. Thomas & J. Grimes (Eds.), *Best practices in school psychology* (Vol. 3, pp. 587–596). Washington, DC: National Association of School Psychologists.

Jensen, E. (2005). *Teaching with the brain in mind* (2nd ed.). Alexandria, VA: ASCD.

Marzano, R., Waters, T., & McNulty, B. A. (2005). *School leadership that works: From research to results.* Alexandria, VA: Association for Supervision and Curriculum Development; Aurora, CO: Mid-continent Research for Education and Learning.

Marzano, R. J. (2003). *What works in schools: Translating research into practice.* Alexandria, VA: ASCD.

Marzano, R. J. (2007). *The art and science of teaching.* Alexandria, VA: ASCD.

Marzano, R. J., Pickering, D. J., & Pollock, J. E. (2001). *Classroom instruction that works.* Alexandria, VA: ASCD.

National Assessment of Educational Progress. (2009). *The nation's report card.* Retrieved from http://nationsreportcard.gov/math_2009/gr4_national.asp

National Council of Teachers of Mathematics. (2005). *Standards and curriculum: A view from the nation.* Washington, DC: Author.

National Council of Teachers of Mathematics. (2006). *Curriculum focal points for prekindergarten through grade 8 mathematics: A quest for coherence.* Washington, DC: Author.

National Mathematics Advisory Council. (2008). *Foundations for success: The final report of the national mathematics advisory council.* Washington, DC: U.S. Department of Education.

Organisation for Economic Co-operation and Development. (2010). *Highlights from Education at a Glance 2010.* Paris, France: Author. doi: 10.1787/eag_highlights-2010-en

Pinnell, G. S. (1989). Reading recovery: Helping at risk children learn to read. *Elementary School Journal, 90,* 161–184.

Romano, A. (2011, March 20). How dumb are we? *Newsweek.* Retrieved from http://www.thedailybeast.com/newsweek/2011/03/20/how-dumb-are-we.html

Schmoker, M., & Marzano, R. J. (1999). Realizing the promise of standards-based education. *Educational Leadership, 56*(6), 17–21.

Sornson, B. (2001). *Preventing early learning failure.* Alexandria, VA: ASCD.

Torgesen, J. K. (2002). The prevention of reading difficulties. *Journal of School Psychology, 40,* 7–26.

U.S. Department of Education, National Center for Education Statistics. (2001). *Entering kindergarten: A portrait of American children when they begin school: Findings from The Condition of Education 2000.* Retrieved from http://nces.ed.gov/pubs2001/2001035.pdf.

U.S. Mint. (2007). *U.S. Mint Presidential Coin Survey.* Washington, DC: Author.

Vygotsky, L. (1978). *Mind in society.* Cambridge, MA: Harvard University Press.

Vygotsky, L. (1986). *Thought and language* (A. Kozulin, Trans. & Ed.). Cambridge, MA: MIT Press.

Ysseldyke, J., Christenson, S., & Thurlow, M. (1987). *Instructional factors that influence student achievement: An integrative review* [Monograph No. 7]. Minneapolis: University of Minnesota Instructional Alternatives Project.

Chapter 3

Ainsworth, L. (2003). *Power standards.* Englewood, CO: Advanced Learning Press.

Common Core State Standards Initiative. (2011). *The standards.* Retrieved from http://www.corestandards.org/the-standards.

Deming, W. E. (1982). *Quality, productivity, and competitive position.* Cambridge, MA: MIT Center for Advanced Engineering Study.

Deming, W. E. (1986). *Out of the crisis.* Cambridge, MA: MIT Center for Advanced Engineering Study.

Deming, W. E. (1993). *The new economics.* Cambridge, MA: MIT Center for Advanced Engineering Study.

Patterson, K., Grenny, J., Maxfield, D., McMillan, R., & Switzler, A. (2008). *Influencer: The power to change anything.* New York, NY: McGraw-Hill.

Schmoker, M., & Marzano, R. J. (1999). Realizing the promise of standards-based education. *Educational Leadership, 56*(6), 17–21.

Chapter 4

Sornson, B. (2012). *Essential skills inventories K–3.* Brighton, MI: Early Learning Foundation.

Chapter 5

Atkin, J. M., Black, P., & Coffey, J. (2001). *Classroom assessment and the national science standards.* Washington, DC: National Academies Press.

Black, P., & Wiliam, D. (1998). Assessment and classroom learning. *Assessment in Education: Principles, Policy and Practice, 5*(1).

Leahy, S., Lyon, C., Thompson, M., & Wiliam, D. (2005). Classroom assessment: Minute-by-minute and day-by-day. *Educational Leadership, 63*(3), 18–24.

Popham, W. J. (2003). *Test better, teach better: The instructional role of assessment.* Alexandria, VA: ASCD.

Reeves, D. B. (2004). *Making standards work: How to implement standards-based assessments in the classroom, school, and district.* Englewood, CO: Advanced Learning Press.

Stiggins, R. (2002). Assessment crisis: The absence of assessment for learning. *Phi Delta Kappan, 90*(6), 419–421. Retrieved from http://www.pdkintl.org/kappan/k0206sti.htm

Stiggins, R., Arter, J., Chappuis, J., & Chappuis, S. (2006). *Classroom assessment for student learning: Doing it right—using it well.* Portland, OR: Educational Testing Service.

Chapter 6

Allington, R. L. (2001). *What really matters for struggling readers: Designing research-based programs.* New York, NY: Longman.

Bailey, B. (2001). *Conscious discipline: 7 Basic skills for brain smart classroom management.* Orlando, FL: Loving Guidance.

Barth, R. (2002). The culture builder. *Educational Leadership, 59*(8), 6–11.

Betts, E. A. (1946). *Foundations of reading instruction.* New York, NY: American Book.

Brophy, J. E., & Evertson, C. M. (1976). *Learning from teaching: a developmental perspective.* Boston, MA: Allyn & Bacon.

Burchinal, M., Kainz, K., Cai, K., Tout, K., Zaslow, M., Martinez-Beck, I., & Rathgeb, C. (2009). *Early care and education quality and child outcomes. Research-to-Policy, Research-to-Practice Brief.* Washington, DC: Office of Planning, Research, and Evaluation, Administration for Children and Families, U.S. Department of Health and Human Services.

Burns, M. K. (2004). Empirical analysis of drill ratio research: Refining the instructional level for drill tasks. *Remedial and Special Education, 25,* 167–175.

Campbell, F. A., Ramey, C. T., Pungello, E. P., Sparling, J., & Miller-Johnson, S. (2002). Early childhood education: Young adult outcomes from the Abecedarian Project. *Applied Developmental Science 6,* 42–57.

Cooke, N. L., & Reichard, S. M. (1996). The effects of different interspersal drill ratios on acquisition and generalization of multiplication and division facts. *Education & Treatment of Children, 19,* 124–142.

Cooke, N. L., Guzaukas, R., Pressley, J. S., & Kerr, K. (1993). Effects of using a ratio of new items to review items during drill and practice: Three experiments. *Education and Treatment of Children, 16,* 212–234.

Emmer, E. T. (1984). *Classroom management: Research and implications.* (R & D Report No. 6178). Austin: Research and Development Center for Teacher Education, University of Texas. Retrieved from ERIC database. (ED251448)

Evertson, C. M., & Emmer, E. T. (1982). Preventive classroom management. In D. Duke (Ed.), *Helping teachers manage classrooms* (pp. 2–31). Alexandria, VA: ASCD.

Fay, J., & Funk, D. (1995). *Teaching with love and logic.* Golden, CO: The Love and Logic Press.

Fuchs, L. S., Fuchs, D., Hamlett, C. L., Hope, S. K., Capizzi, A. M., Craddock, C. F., & Brothers, B. L. (2006). Extending responsiveness-to-intervention to math problem solving at third grade. *Teaching Exceptional Children, 38*(4), 59–63.

Gettinger, M., & Seibert, J. K. (2002). Best practices in increasing academic learning time. In A. Thomas & J. Grimes (Eds.), *Best practices in school psychology* (Vol. 4, pp. 773–787). Bethesda, MD: The National Association of School Psychologists.

Gickling, E. E., & Armstrong, D. L. (1978). Levels of instructional difficulty as related to on-task behavior, task completion, and comprehension. *Journal of Learning Disabilities, 11,* 32–39.

Gickling, E. E., & Rosenfield, S. (1995). Best practices in curriculum-based assessment. In A. Thomas & J. Grimes (Eds.), *Best practices in school psychology* (Vol. 3, pp. 587–596). Washington, DC: National Association of School Psychologists.

Gickling, E. E., & Thompson, V. P. (1985). A personal view of curriculum-based assessment. *Exceptional Children, 52*(3), 205–218.

Glasser, W. (1969). *Schools without failure.* New York, NY: Harper and Row.

Glasser, W. (1990). *The quality school: Managing students without coercion.* New York, NY: Harper and Row.

Glasser, W. (1998). *Choice theory in the classroom.* New York, NY: Harper Perennial.

Kriete, R. (2002). *The morning meeting book.* Turner Falls, MA: Northeast Foundation for Children.

MacQuarrie, L. L., Tucker, J. A., Burns, M. K., & Hartman, B. (2002). Comparison of retention rates using traditional, Drill Sandwich, and Incremental Rehearsal flashcard methods. *School Psychology Review, 31,* 584–595.

Marzano, R. J. (2003). *What works in schools.* Alexandria, VA: ASCD.

Marzano, R. J., & Marzano, J. S. (2003). The key to classroom management. *Educational Leadership, 61*(1), 6–13.

Marzano, R. J. (with Marzano, J. S., & Pickering, D. J.). (2003). *Classroom management that works.* Alexandria, VA: ASCD.

Marzano, R. J., Pickering, D. J., & Pollock, J. E. (2001). Classroom instruction that works: Research based strategies for increasing student achievement. Alexandria, VA: ASCD.

Pinnell, G. S. (1989). Reading recovery: Helping at risk children learn to read. *Elementary School Journal, 90,* 161–184.

Roberts, M. L., & Shapiro, E. S. (1996). Effects of instructional ratios on students' reading performance in a regular education program. *Journal of School Psychology, 34,* 73–91.

Rosenberg, M. (2003). Nonviolent communication: A language of life. *School Psychology Review, 36,* 159–166.

Schweinhart, L. J., Barnes, H. V., & Weikart, D. P. (1993). *Significant benefits: The High/Scope Perry preschool study through age 27* (Monographs of the HighScope Educational Research Foundation, 10). Ypsilanti, MI: HighScope Press.

Sornson, B. (2001). *Preventing early learning failure.* Alexandria, VA: ASCD.

Sternberg, R. J., & Grigorenko, E. L. (2004). Successful intelligence in the classroom. *Theory Into Practice, 43*(4), 274–280.

Stipek, D. J. (1996). Motivation and instruction. In D. C. Berliner & R. C. Calfee (Eds.), *Handbook of educational psychology* (pp. 85–113). New York, NY: Simon Schuster Macmillan.

Torgesen, J. K. (2002). The prevention of reading difficulties. *Journal of School Psychology, 40,* 7–26.

Treptow, M. A., Burns, M. K., & McComas, J. J. (2007). Reading at the frustration, instructional, and independent levels: Effects of student time on task and comprehension. *School Psychology Review, 36,* 159–166.

Wong, Harry K., & Wong, R. (2009). *The first days of school: How to be an effective teacher.* Mountain View, GA: Harry K. Wong Publications.

Ysseldyke, J., Christenson, S., & Thurlow, M. (1987). *Instructional factors that influence student achievement: An integrative review* [Monograph No. 7]. Minneapolis: University of Minnesota Instructional Alternatives Project.

Chapter 7

Aksamit, D. L., & Rankin, J. L. (1993). Problem-solving teams as a prereferral process. *Special Services in the Schools, 7,* 1–25.

Allington, R. (2005). *What really matters for struggling readers.* Boston, MA: Allyn & Bacon.

Allington, R. (2008). *What really matters in response to intervention.* Boston, MA: Allyn & Bacon.

Association for Quality and Participation. (2008). International team excellence award showcases collaborative problem solving. *The Journal for Quality and Participation, 31*(2), 33–38

Chalfant, J. C., Pysh, V., & Moltrie, R. (1979). Teacher assistance teams: A model for within-building problem solving. *Learning Disability Quarterly, 2*, 85–96.

Fuchs, D., Mock, D., Morgan, P. L., & Young, C. L. (2003). Responsiveness-to-intervention: Definitions, evidence, and implications for the learning disabilities construct. *Learning Disabilities Research & Practice, 18*(3), 157–171.

Fuchs, D., Fuchs, L. S., & Bahr, M. W. (1990). Mainstream assistance teams: A scientific basis for the art of consultation. *Exceptional Children, 57*, 128–139.

Hessler, G. (2001). Who is really learning disabled? In B. Sornson (Ed.), *Preventing early learning failure* (pp. 21–36). Alexandria, VA: ASCD.

Katzenbach, J. R., & Smith, D. K. (1993). *the wisdom of teams: Creating the high performance organization.* Boston, MA: Harvard Business School Press.

Kovaleski, J. F., & Glew, M. C. (2006). Bringing instructional support teams to scale: Implications of the Pennsylvania experience. *Remedial and Special Education, 27*, 16–25.

Kovaleski, J. F., Tucker, J. A., & Stevens, L. J. (1996). Bridging special and regular education: The Pennsylvania initiative. *Educational Leadership, 53*(5), 44–47.

Kruger, L. J. (1997). Social support and self-efficacy in problem solving among teacher assistance teams and school staff. *The Journal of Educational Research, 90*(3), 164–168.

Marchington, M. (1992). *Managing the team: A guide to successful employee involvement.* Oxford, England: Blackwell.

McGlothlin, J. E. (1981). The school consultation committee: An approach to implementing a teacher consultation model. *Behavioral Disorders, 6*, 101–107.

Mills, E. (2007). *Meet Google's culture czar.* Retrieved from http://www.zdnet .com.au/insight/software/soa/Meet-Google-s-culture-czar/0,139023769, 339275147,00.htm.

Moore, K. J., Fifield, M. B., Spira, D. A., & Scarlato, M. (1989). Child study team decision making in special education: Improving the process. *Remedial and Special Education, 10*(4), 50–58.

Newman, D. S. (2007). *An investigation of the effect of instructional consultation teams on special education placement rate.* Dissertation abstract, University of Maryland. Retrieved from http://drum.lib.umd.edu/bitstream/1903/7772/ 1/umi-umd-5054.pdf

Rebora, A. (2010, April 12). Responding to RTI (interview with Dick Allington). *Education Week Teacher PD Sourcebook.* Retrieved from http://www.edweek. org/tsb/articles/2010/04/12/02allington.h03.html

Rosenfield, S., & Gravois, T.A. (1996). *Instructional consultation teams: Collaborating for change.* New York, NY: Guilford Press.

Saver, K., & Downes, B. (1991). PIT crew: A model for teacher collaboration in an elementary school. *Intervention in School and Clinic, 27*, 116–120.

Senge, P. M. (2006). *The fifth discipline: The art and practice of the learning organization.* New York, NY: Doubleday Publishing.

Senge, P. M., Cambron-McCabe, N., Lucas, T., Smith, B., Dutton, J., & Kleiner, A. (2000). *Schools that learn: A fifth discipline fieldbook for educators, parents, and everyone who cares about education.* New York, NY: Doubleday Publishing.

Sornson, B. (2001). *Preventing early learning failure.* Alexandria, VA: ASCD.

Sornson, B. (2007). The early learning success initiative. *Educational Leadership, 65*(2), 42–43.

Sornson, B., Frost, F., & Burns, M. (2005). Instructional support teams in Michigan, *Communique, 33*(5), 28–29.

Chapter 8

Barnett, W. S. (1996). *Lives in the balance: Age-27 benefit-cost analysis of the HighScope Perry Preschool Program* (Monographs of the HighScope Educational Research Foundation, 11). Ypsilanti, MI: HighScope Press.

Barnett, W. S. (2011, August 19). Mend it, don't end it [Web log message]. Retrieved from http://preschoolmatters.org/2011/08/19/head-start-mend-it-don%E2%80%99t-end-it/

Barnett, W. S., et al. (2010). *The state of preschool yearbook, 2010.* New Brunswick, NJ: Rutgers University.

Barnett, W. S. (2011). Effectiveness of early educational intervention. *Science, 333*(6045), 975–978.

Barnett, W. S., Lamy, C., & Kwanghee, J. (2005). *The effects of state prekindergarten program on young children's school readiness in five states.* Brunswick, NJ: National Institute for Early Education Research.

Bartik, T. (2011). *Investing in kids: Early childhood programs and local economic development.* Kalamazoo, MI: W.E. Upjohn Institute for Employment Research.

Bowman, B. T., Donovan, M. S., & Burns, M.S. (2001). *Eager to learn: Educating our preschoolers.* Washington, DC: National Academy Press.

Burchinal, M. R., Campbell, F. A., Bryant, D. M., Wasik, B. H., & Ramey, C. T. (1997). Early intervention and mediating processes in cognitive performance of children of low-income African American families. *Child Development, 68*(5), 935–954.

Campbell, F. A., Pungello, E. P., Miller-Johnson, S., Burchinal, M., & Ramey, C. T. (2001). The development of cognitive and academic abilities: Growth curves from an early childhood educational experiment, *Developmental Psychology, 37*(2), 231–242.

Deming, D. (2009). Early childhood intervention and life-cycle skill development: evidence from Head Start. *American Economic Journal: Applied Economics, 1*(3), 111–134.

Foundation for Child Development. (2008). *America's vanishing potential: The case for preK–3rd education.* New York, NY: Foundation for Child Development.

Garces, E., Duncan T., & Currie, J. (2002). Longer-term effects of Head Start. *American Economic Review, 92*(4), 999–1012.

Hart, B., & Risley, T. (1995). *Meaningful differences in the everyday experience of young American children.* Baltimore, MD: Brookes.

Heckman, J. J., & Masterov, D. V. (2007). The productivity argument for investing in young children. *Review of Agricultural Economics, 29,* 446–493.

Hernandez, D. (2011). *Double jeopardy: How third-grade reading skills and poverty influence high school graduation.* Baltimore, MD: Annie E. Casey Foundation.

Johnson, R. C. (2010). *School quality and the long-run effects of Head Start.* (IRP Thematic Seminar series). Retrieved from http://www.sole-jole.org/12440.pdf

Karoly, L. A., Kilburn, M.R., & Cannon, J. S. (2005). *Proven benefits of early childhood interventions.* Santa Monica, CA: RAND Corporation. Retrieved from http://www.rand.org/pubs/research_briefs/RB9145

Klein, J. (2011, July 7). Time to ax public programs that don't yield results. *Time* pp. 6–7. Retrieved from http://www.time.com/time/nation/article/0,8599,2081778,00.html#ixzz1UqSuspUQ

Mead, S. (2008). *Partners in closing the achievement gap.* New York, NY: Democrats for Education Reform. Retrieved from http://www.dfer.org/prek/dfer-prek-briefing.pdf

Office of Planning, Research and Evaluation Administration for Children and Families, U.S. Department of Health and Human Services. (2010). *Head Start research study, final report.* Washington, DC: Author.

Organisation for Economic Co-operation and Development. (2010). *Education at a glance: OECD indicators 2010.* Paris, France: Author.

Risley, T. R., & Hart, B. (1995). *Meaningful differences in the everyday experience of young American children.* Baltimore, MD: Brookes.

Schweinhart, L. J., Montie, J., Xiang, Z., Barnett, W. S., Belfield, C. R., & Nores, M. (2005). *Lifetime effects: The HighScope Perry Preschool study through age 40.* (Monographs of the HighScope Educational Research Foundation, 14). Ypsilanti, MI: HighScope Press.

Shonkoff, J. P., & Phillips, D. A. (2000). *From neurons to neighborhoods: The science of early childhood development.* Washington, DC: National Academy Press.

Shore, R. (2009). *The case for investing in preK–3rd education: Challenging myths about school reform.* New York, NY: Foundation for Child Development.

Snyder, R. (2011). *Special address to legislature, April 2011.* Retrieved from http://www.michigan.gov/documents/snyder/SpecialMessageonEducationReform_351586_7.pdf

Sornson, B. (2007). The early learning success initiative. *Educational Leadership, 65*(2), 42–43.

Sornson, B., Frost, F., & Burns, M. (2005). Instructional support teams in Michigan. *Communique, 33*(5), 28–29.

U.S. Census Bureau. (2011). *POV01: Age and sex of all people, family members and unrelated individuals iterated by income-to-poverty ratio and race: 2010.* Retrieved from http://www.census.gov/hhes/www/cpstables/032011/pov/new01_200_01.htm

U.S. Department of Health and Human Services, Administration for Children and Families. (2010). *Head Start impact study: Final report.* Retrieved from http://www.acf.hhs.gov/programs/opre/hs/impact_study/reports/impact_study/hs_impact_study_final.pdf

Weikart, D., Bond, J. T., & McNeil, J. T. (1978). *The Ypsilanti Perry Preschool Project.* Ypsilanti, MI: HighScope.

Whitehurst, G. J. (2011, January 21). Is Head Start working for American students? [Web log message]. Retrieved from http://www.brookings.edu/opinions/2010/0121_head_start_whitehurst.aspx

Zorn, D., Noga, J., Bolden-Haraway, C., Louis, V., Owens, N., & Smith, S. (2004). *Family poverty and its implications for school success.* Cincinnati, OH: University of Cincinnati Evaluation Services Center.

Chapter 9

Baker, A. J., & Sodden, L. M. (1997). *Parent involvement in children's education: A critical assessment of the knowledge base.* Paper presented at the annual meeting of the American Educational Research Association, Chicago, Illinois.

de Bruyn, E. H., Deković, M., & Meijnen, G. W. (2003). Parenting, goal orientations, classroom behavior, and school success in early adolescence. *Applied Developmental Psychology, 24,* 393–412.

Fay, C. (2008). *Love and Logic insider's club.* Golden: Love and Logic Institute.

Finn, Jeremy D. 1998. *Class size and students at risk: What is known? What is next?* Washington, DC: U.S. Department of Education, Office of Educational Research and Improvement, National Institute on the Education of At-Risk Students.

Henderson, A. T., & Berla, N. (Eds.). (1994). *A new generation of evidence: The family is critical to student achievement.* Columbia, MD: National Committee for Citizens in Education.

Hoy, W. K., & Tschannen-Moran, M. (2003). The conceptualization and measurement of faculty trust in schools: The omnibus T-Scale. In W. K. Hoy & C. Miskel (Eds.), *Studies in leading and organizing schools* (pp. 181–208). Greenwich CT: Information Age.

Kellaghan, T., Sloane, K., Alvarez, B., & Bloom, B. S. (1993). *The home environment and school learning: Promoting parental involvement in the education of children.* San Francisco, CA: Jossey-Bass.

Lee, V. E., & Croninger, R. G. (1994). The relative importance of home and school in the development of literacy skills for middle-grade students. *American Journal of Education, 102*(3), 286–329.

Ramey, S. L., & Ramey, C. T. (1999). *Going to School: How to help your child succeed: a handbook for parents of children 3 to 8.* New York, NY: Goddard Press.

Reynolds, A. J., Temple J. A., Robertson, D. L., & Mann, E. A. (2001). *Age 21 cost-benefit analysis of the Title I Chicago child-parent center program.* Washington, DC: National Institute of Child Health and Human Development.

Seligman, M. (2004). *Authentic happiness.* New York, NY: Free Press.

Sornson, B. (2012). *Parent empowerment program.* Inkster, MI: Starfish Family Services.

Tschannen-Moran, M. (2003). Fostering organizational citizenship: Transformational leadership and trust. In W. K. Hoy & C. G. Miskel, *Studies in Leading and Organizing Schools* (pp. 157–179). Greenwich, CT: Information Age.

Tough, P. (2008). *Whatever it takes: Geoffrey Canada's quest to change Harlem and America.* Boston, MA: Houghton Mifflin Harcourt.

Zygmunt-Fillwalk, E. (2006). Encouraging school success through family involvement. *Childhood Education, 82*(4), 226–F.

Chapter 10

Milgram, S. (1963). Behavioral study of obedience. *Journal of Abnormal and Social Psychology, 67*(4), 371–378.

Milgram, S. (1974). *Obedience to authority: An experimental view.* New York, NY: Harper Collins.

Chapter 11

Barnett, W. S. (1996). *Lives in the balance: Age-27 benefit-cost analysis of the HighScope Perry Preschool Program* (Monographs of the HighScope Educational Research Foundation, 11). Ypsilanti, MI: HighScope Press.

Burchinal, M. R., Campbell, F. A., Bryant, D. M., Wasik, B. H., & Ramey, C. T. (1997). Early intervention and mediating processes in cognitive performance of children of low-income African American Families. *Child Development, 68*(5), 935–954.

Cadwell, L. B. (2002). *Bringing learning to life: A Reggio approach to early childhood education.* New York, NY: Teachers College Press.

Campbell, F. A., Pungello, E. P., Miller-Johnson, S., Burchinal, M., & Ramey, C. T. (2001). The development of cognitive and academic abilities: Growth curves from an early childhood educational experiment. *Developmental Psychology, 37*(2), 231–242.

The Early Childhood Initiative Foundation. (2011, December 2). David Lawrence Jr. speech to the annual gathering of the Florida School Boards Association and the Superintendents Association, Tampa, FL. Retrieved from http://www.teachmorelovemore.org/Speeches.asp?speechid=

Heckman, J. (2011). *Letter to Joint Select Committee on deficit reduction.* Retrieved from the Heckman: The Economics of Human Potential website: http://www.heckmanequation.org/content/resource/letter-joint-select-committee-deficit-reduction

Lewin-Benham, A. (2008). *Powerful children: Understanding how to think and learn using the Reggio approach.* New York, NY: Teachers College Press.

Newhill, S. L. (1992). *The Early Childhood Development Program, 1991–1992, summative evaluation* (pp. 1–63). Kansas City, MO: Evaluation Office—Desegregation Planning Department, Kansas City, Missouri School District.

Sahlberg, P. (2011). *Finnish lessons.* New York, NY: Teachers College Press.

Schweinhart, L. J., Montie, J., Xiang, Z., Barnett, W. S., Belfield, C. R., & Nores, M. (2005). *Lifetime effects: The HighScope Perry Preschool study through age 40.* (Monographs of the HighScope Educational Research Foundation, 14). Ypsilanti, MI: HighScope Press.

Slavin, R. E., Karweit, N. L., & Wasik, B. A. (1992). Preventing early school failure: What works? *Education Leadership, 50*(4).

Tough, P. (2008). *Whatever it takes: Geoffrey Canada's quest to change Harlem and America.* Boston, MA: Houghton Mifflin Harcourt.

Wagner, M., & Clayton, S. L. (2001). The Parents as Teachers program: Results from two demonstrations. *The Future of Children, 9,* 91–115.

Weikart, D., Bond, J. T., & McNeil, J. T. (1978). *The Ypsilanti Perry Preschool Project.* Ypsilanti, MI: HighScope.

Chapter 12

Anderson, R. C., Wilson, P. T., & Fielding, L. G. (1988). Growth in reading and how children spend time outside of school. *Reading Research Quarterly, 23,* 285–303.

Hawking, S. W. (1988). *A brief history of time.* New York, NY: Bantam Books.

Huxley, A. (1930). *Vulgarity in literature: Digressions from a theme.* London, England: Chatto & Windus.

Jacobs, G. M., & Crowley, K. E. (2007). *Play, projects and preschool standards: Nurturing children's sense of wonder and joy in learning.* Thousand Oaks, CA: Corwin.

Maslow, A. (1954). *Motivation and personality.* New York, NY: Harper.

Salomon, G., & Globerson, T. (1987). Skill may not be enough: The role of mindfulness in learning and transfer. *International Journal of Educational Research, 11,* 623–637.

Strickland, K., & Walker, A. (2004). "Re-valuing" reading: Assessing attitude and providing appropriate reading support. *Reading and Writing Quarterly, 20,* 401–418.

Torgesen, J. (2004). Preventing early reading failure—and its devastating downward spiral: The evidence for early intervention. *American Educator. 28,* 6–19.

Torgesen, J. K. (1998). Catch them before they fall. *American Educator, 22*(1–2), 32–39.

Chapter 14

Annie E. Casey Foundation. (2010) *Early warning! Why reading by the end of third grade matters.* Baltimore, MD: Author.

Hernandez, D. (2011). *Double jeopardy: How third-grade reading skills and poverty influence high school graduation.* Baltimore, MD: Annie E. Casey Foundation.

Shaywitz, B. A., Shaywitz, S. E., Fletcher, J. M., Pugh, K. R., Gore, J. C., Constable, R. T., . . . Lacadie, C. (1997). The Yale Center for the Study of Learning and Attention: Longitudinal and neurobiological studies. *Learning Disabilities: A Multidisciplinary Journal, 8,* 21–30.

Wilson, F. (2011, October 25). Fred Wilson blog. Retrieved from http://www.avc.com

Index

CORWIN
A SAGE Company

The Corwin logo—a raven striding across an open book—represents the union of courage and learning. Corwin is committed to improving education for all learners by publishing books and other professional development resources for those serving the field of PreK–12 education. By providing practical, hands-on materials, Corwin continues to carry out the promise of its motto: **"Helping Educators Do Their Work Better."**